Sincere Wishes

Willis Reed

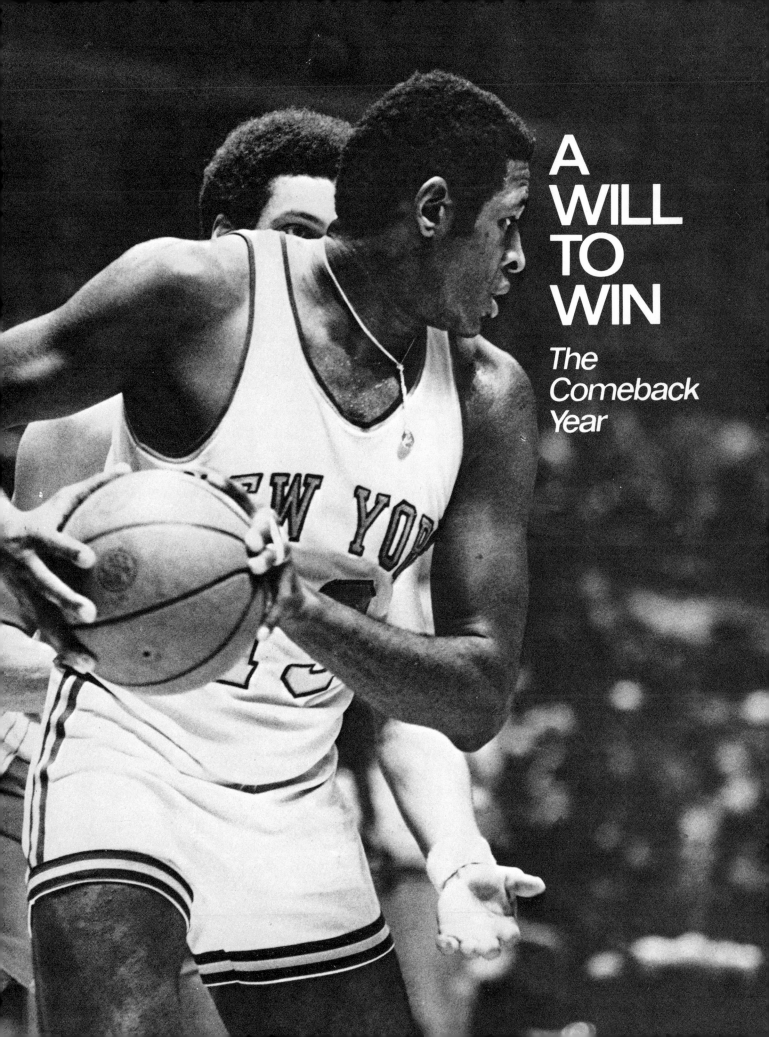

A WILL TO WIN

The Comeback Year

A WILL TO WIN
The Comeback Year

by
Willis Reed

Photography by
George Kalinsky

A Stuart L. Daniels Book

PRENTICE-HALL, INC.
Englewood Cliffs, New Jersey

A Stuart L. Daniels Production

With deep appreciation for the editorial assistance of Lew Fishman.

A WILL TO WIN
The Comeback Year

By Willis Reed
With George Kalinsky

Published by Prentice-Hall, Inc.
Englewood Cliffs, New Jersey

Printed in the United States of America • T

Prentice-Hall International, Inc., London
Prentice-Hall of Australia, Pty. Ltd., Sydney
Prentice-Hall of Canada, Ltd., Toronto
Prentice-Hall of India Private Ltd., New Delhi
Prentice-Hall of Japan, Inc., Tokyo

ISBN 0-13-959791-3
Library of Congress Catalog Card No. 73-90644

Willis Reed is more than a basketball player; he is an unusually warm human being.

Those of us who are fortunate enough to work with Willis know his aptitude to play basketball is outweighed by Willis Reed, The Man.

George Kalinsky

INTRODUCTION

I have known Willis Reed for many years, and have always been impressed by his sensitivity, generosity and humility.

I have followed his career with great interest and have watched him grow into a magnificent athlete. On the court Willis's determination and enthusiastic leadership is a great inspiration to his teammates. His unrelenting will enabled him to overcome the frustration and anguish of an injury that threatened to end his career. He is truly a man among men.

J. Walter Kennedy
Commissioner, National Basketball
Association

Frustration...
Helplessness

There's nothing with which I can compare it . . . that feeling of frustration . . . the helplessness . . . the inability to contribute.

Here it was staring me right in the face. After eleven regular season games in 1971, I was standing there in the middle of the Garden and the realization was slowly coming on that I just wasn't being of any help to the team.

I had a tough time rebounding with the other centers. My moves toward the basket were not deceiving anyone. My quickness both on offense and defense was all but gone.

I had been playing with injuries and pain for many years, but this was the low point, and by November 11, 1971 I knew I just couldn't go on. The injury of my thigh in the two previous years and the physical punishment I had taken since I came into the tough National Basketball Association had taken their toll.

All I could think of was to get off someplace all by myself and think things out.

I had been playing for many years with injury and pain . . . Now, I knew I couldn't go on.

Basketball had been my life since I was thirteen. For almost twenty years it had been an all-consuming passion. I was proud to be the captain of the Knicks but I also realized that the honor carried responsibilities with it as well. If I couldn't keep up with the other fellows, if I couldn't provide the leadership a team's captain should, then perhaps it would be better if I stepped aside completely. But I'm not a quitter and that would be quitting. I had to overcome this problem; I had to fight it.

We were facing the Golden State Warriors that night. I was ready for my usual matchup against Nate Thurmond, one of the best centers in the game and always a challenge. And then the awful, grinding pain.

From that November 11, 1971 until October 21, 1972, I was not able to play in a regular game with the Knicks. The pain in my knee and leg continued and while the doctors never said so specifically, it was apparent that there was much to do and be done before I could return to the game.

While I didn't realize all this at that moment, as I sat alone in the dressing room, I sensed that there were to be changes in my life. Medical consultations in the weeks ahead made the situation more specific.

I sat there asking questions of myself, almost like a quizmaster . . . and found only I could answer my queries.

I've always believed that everything has to be looked at from the bright side, from a positive angle. I could never let the doubt creep into my mind that I might not finish the job of helping take the Knicks on to another championship. There really couldn't be any other answer. I'm not that type of person.

Sitting in that lonely dressing room after I had limped off the court, I began to think about my past life. I guess I had always known fear or apprehension in one way or another but I've always tried to battle it. It does make winning that much sweeter.

It's like when I first took up basketball. I was the tallest kid in school and probably the worst player. But the coach went out of his way to help me.

I tried out for the team, and although I knew my ability was limited to size, he told me I had the potential. So I went out there and I never let up . . . from the time he put a basketball in my hands. It took a lot of work. I found you had to develop mentally as well as physically. It helps, but you're still scared.

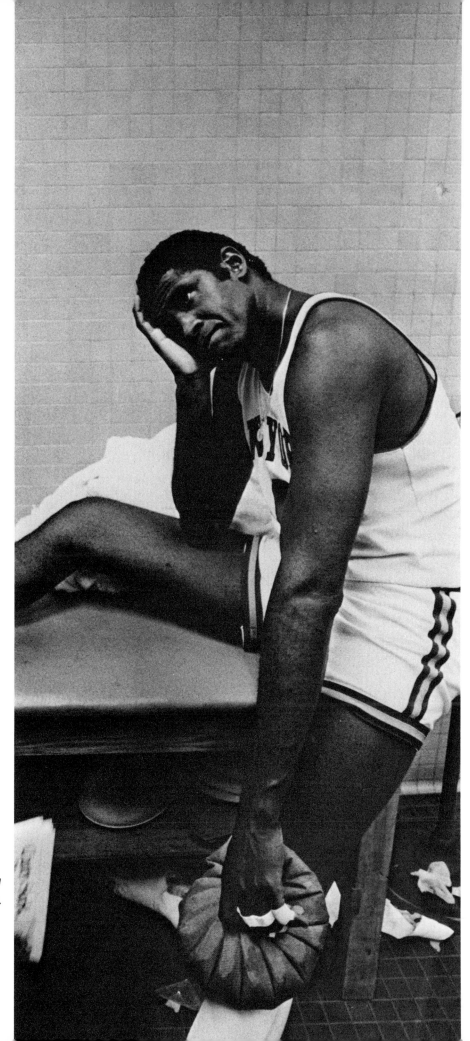

I sat alone in the dressing room and sensed there would be changes in my life.

It's a long walk through the corridor, especially
when you are alone and injured.

In my first game I was frightened to death. That's the honest to God truth. I was in the ninth grade. The coach put me into the lineup and I scored four points. I was scared all through the game.

The next time out, I got only two points, and I began thinking I'm getting worse, and man, when you score only four points to begin with, getting worse is sure going to cause some concern.

In the next game I went out and did what the coach had been teaching me all along. It seemed like everything was coming together. I scored twenty-three points. I have to admit I was still apprehensive.

Things that happen in basketball mirror life in many ways. To this day, when I step out on the court, I still have that fear of the unknown . . . and I worry. I'll look at the center I'm meeting and I think this guy is really good. I'll have to be at the peak of my game tonight if we're going to win. I can't take a chance of underestimating him at any time. I must stay alert—I can't be lackadaisical.

Out on the court you can't let down for even a minute, because you know that you'll be taken advantage of, and that you'll be, in effect, beating yourself. Well, that's a pretty big part of life in general.

I didn't let up when I was a kid and I certainly wasn't going to start doing something different now.

The tendonitis in my knee had been limiting my play. It could have been the end of my career.

I wasn't going to let it get the better of me. It was a fight . . . another bout with one of life's problems, and fear was the greatest obstacle.

If you let these anxieties get to you, there's no way you can come out a winner. It's one strike and you're out, instead of going for the full three.

I've seen a lot of kids doing that. When they meet disappointment, they don't come back. You can't fall down once and feel you're not ever going to get up. You have to overcome the obstacles in your path. Summon your strength; condense it into one powerful package . . . get your mind and your body functioning together at optimum efficiency. And that's the only way you're going to come out ahead of the game, whether it's basketball or life itself.

In the fifth game of the 1970 championship series against the Los Angeles Lakers, I found myself on the floor of the court in great pain.

16

I returned in time for the seventh and last—the winning game, and received a standing ovation from the crowd.

For want of any better term, I call this determination "the will to win." I really feel it's the most essential ingredient for success in life. It has to be developed, cultivated, nurtured in the home and community from earliest childhood. This is where a man draws his inner strength, where he gets the ability to jump over the hurdles which are placed before him whether on purpose or by accident.

Most people are looking for crutches. They try to find a way out with alibis. They'll blame everybody else for their own failures. I am just fortunate . . . I never was dependent on a lot of other people.

We are all products of our environments. You can't escape it. I grew up in a rural area of the South, in Louisiana. I had to work hard to provide necessities for myself. If I needed a pair of shoes I couldn't go to my father and ask for them. He'd only tell me to get out and work to buy the shoes myself if I needed them so badly. He didn't have any money. He worked hard but the pay was low.

Kids today have it very different. I see them in New York plopping down fifty-dollar bills that came right out of Pop's billfold.

In contrast, I go out at night onto the basketball floor and give everything I can for a schedule of more than 100 games, including exhibitions and playoffs. By the end of the season, I'm pretty exhausted. I guess all of us are.

But being able to do this, to give of myself, makes me more fortunate than a lot of others. It's a greater feeling to have than the one the kid has who hasn't done anything more than count his papa's change. All that kid has to look forward to is another night of hanging around gas stations and hamburger joints, showing off the clothes he's bought with his parents' money.

I earned whatever I received. I was a bit more independent from the start, because of my family's circumstances. But I really began to mature and gain some insight into life when I started playing basketball.

I had to learn to give . . . that's not an easy thing to do, but it can be fantastically rewarding. You learn that every man on the football team can't be the quarterback . . . not every player on a basketball team can be the high scorer. Each team member has a job to do, and if it's done the right way, and if the ability and the determination are there, no matter what you do, you won't have to take a back seat to anybody.

In high school and college I worked my butt off at basketball, putting in long hours, but they were gratifying hours. I wanted to play and I was willing to sacrifice a good many things to get what I wanted. When you speak to players and coaches, businessmen and professional men, you'll find that the ones who have become successful have sacrificed a good deal in their lives.

I knew all of this. I had taken my share of lumps, but now I had a knot in my stomach and my knee was aching.

None of the guys on the Knicks said anything. They treated me with a great degree of respect. Here I was, the captain of the team, performing far below par . . . maybe even hurting the team's chances, because we had Jerry Lucas sitting on the bench. It was a tough pill to swallow.

At night when I lay down, the pain was so excruciating, I couldn't think straight . . . I was in no frame of mind to analyze my situation. But that is what I was forced to do. I knew that I must make a decision . . . and it was the most difficult decision I'd ever be called upon to make.

In retrospect I think that the injury which almost cut my career short has made me a better man. I am now able to evaluate myself objectively. Many people are unable to evaluate and analyze their position in life. Without such objective analysis, one often comes up with absurd conclusions. When I looked at myself in proper perspective, I definitely knew where I stood. Although it didn't exactly look good for my future as a basketball player, I was still able to deal with my situation as a man more effectively.

In essence, what it comes down to is that you must make a commitment to yourself and understand that you have a responsibility to bear. I have always felt I was obligated to various people. I believed that I owed the Knicks, as well as my coaches in college and high school, a continuing commitment to do my best. They had always believed in me. That was a great incentive to keep me going.

In a certain sense I started out to prove something . . . that I was the best at whatever job at which I worked. There were many who stuck by me and sacrificed for me. All along the way they made certain goals possible for me to attain. These are the people to whom I will forever feel indebted. And now I was being called on to pay back a bit of what I had gained from their willingness to help.

All that's ever really been asked of me is to give whatever I had, both as a ballplayer and as a man. I hope that I've succeeded in making my benefactors proud.

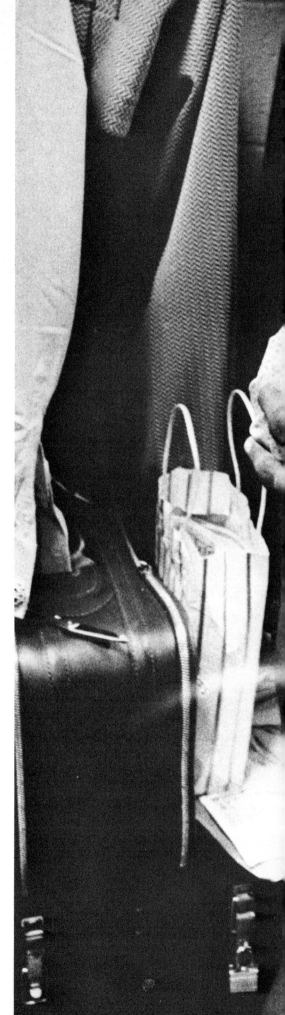

I have been playing with injuries throughout my career.

A reporter once asked, "What would you want written about you as a ballplayer after your playing days are over?"

My answer was really very simple. If just one thing was to be written about me, I'd like it to be, "Willis Reed gave 100 percent of what he had all the time." They don't have to write that I was the greatest ballplayer in the world. When a man gives 100 percent as a ballplayer and as a man, there's nothing else that can be asked of him. And he must be considered successful in his own eyes and those of others.

That's probably why I am my own best critic. Since I know Willis Reed better than anyone else, I'm constantly questioning whether I have given enough of myself. Usually, I feel I could have given more.

Many times before a game, I've been so tired physically that I couldn't even conceive of playing. I'd sit on the bench in front of my locker and psych myself up. I also would ask the Lord to give me the strength to play forty-eight minutes of basketball.

It always works. Some of the greatest games I've played in my life have come after this inward look and personal pep talk. The mental aspect of a person completely dominates his physical attributes. It has been proven time and again that people who really have the desire and the persistence to follow up will do things others could not hope to achieve.

Sometimes this strength and determination come through anger. If I get mad at myself, I'll push and drive that much harder. In that sense I think anger can be called a positive emotion.

No matter how well you do something, whatever status you've attained, you should reach further. Robert Browning wrote in the 19th century, ". . . a man's reach should exceed his grasp." I believe in that strongly. It's what makes all of us keep coming back, giving that extra effort, extending ourselves to the fullest.

I remember, in high school, when our team had a bad year. Almost every time we played, we lost. That's when I discovered that losing can also have a positive function. Sometimes you get so tired of losing that you work doubly hard to come home with a victory.

That year, when I'd come home from the game around ten or eleven o'clock, my mother would ask me who won. It got to be so bad I could hardly face her. I guess she already knew we'd been beaten.

But we didn't quit. By the end of my sophomore high school year, the team was really beginning to blossom. And I was playing with a lot more assurance and confidence. It took a while, but I believe that one losing season made our ball club better in the long run.

Maybe our troubles today could be eased by instilling a sense of pride in all young people. Personal pride is essential. It is a catalyst which helps carry one towards his goals.

I believe I have a good deal of this in me. It is one of the reasons I could not let myself throw away everything I had attained.

Around this time, newspaper sports columnists were writing that I was through as a player, and that I should quit. I sat down and considered their words. My mind kept coming back to the same conclusion.

How could these people, without formal medical training, or even a knowledge of the extent of my injury, make rash judgments. The doctors themselves were having trouble in trying to diagnose my ailment and prescribe treatment. Yet here I was being written off by these reporters. I won't say it didn't bother me, but it did make me more determined than ever to prove them wrong.

I had had to foresake too many pleasant things in life; I had had to discipline my mind and my body to get where I was. I wasn't going to walk out and say good-bye to basketball at the suggestion of a few writers.

However, if my decision turned out to be wrong, if I was mistaken and wasn't able to do well, I think I would be man enough to admit it.

Funny thing, the doctors never really came out and said, "Willis, you have to give up playing basketball. You can't do this or you can't do that." They had told me during the 1970–71 season that I couldn't do any more harm to my knee by running and jumping. It was already so painful.

If the medical men figured that way, then I decided I was going to play. That year I wound up with more minutes of game action than in any of the previous NBA seasons. Sure, I was in anguish most of the time. I realize that a good many other players wouldn't do the same thing, but I was of the opinion that I had to do it for the team.

Between ball games, I'd try to grab a couple of days of rest and afterwards I'd feel really good. I'd play fairly well

until the end of the game, by which time I'd seem to lose my ability to move. The only thing I could say about that was that I was giving my best. And I know the guys on the club, like Bill Bradley and Dave DeBusschere and Clyde (Walt Frazier) and Dick Barnett, everyone, appreciated it. They never told me so but I knew.

Even though we didn't win the championship that year, I received some satisfaction because we had a really close-knit team. I'm sure that every member did the best he could, but, unfortunately, it wasn't enough . . . that year.

I always remember that life is more losing than winning. In one's lifetime there'll be countless more failures than successes. But that makes victory when it comes so much more glorious.

Take the situation in the National Basketball Association, which has seventeen teams. Granted, not all of them are great clubs, but there are a goodly number of outstanding organizations. Yet, when all is said and done, at the close of the season there can be only one champion. Some finish better than others. A few reach the playoffs and only two get into the final round, but where it's really all at is that it's just one team that has the honor of being champions.

They usually don't write too much about the losers in the playoffs. They concentrate on the team that won. But the other sixteen were trying. All anyone can ever do is to give his best whenever he is called on.

I think a good deal about the kids who are playing basketball in high school now. Those boys are going to be the All-Staters of the future. Some of them are going to move on to college and some of those will become All-Americans. There'll be another large group. They won't even have the opportunity to attend a university or college.

But of all those young boys who go on to college and participate in intercollegiate sports, how many will become established, nationally recognized players? How many will become All-Americans and be drafted into the professional ranks? How many will actually be able to stick with NBA teams, and of those who do come through, how many will be superstars?

Very few—very few, indeed. But that doesn't mean they can't be successful in other fields. I like to think that athletics builds character in a person. Even at the high school level, competition can be as fierce as it is in the NBA.

The pains continued to mount and when I felt faint during the Warrior game, I was in a state of limbo.

At one point when I was out for several months there was some talk about my becoming a coach, but I have a stubborn streak. Maybe if I wasn't so rigid I might have considered it, since I was having trouble negotiating a contract anyway. I think some other ballplayers would have gone for a slightly lesser salary, but I felt I was going to recover, and if I was going to play, I asked for what I believed was fair and just. And the Knicks have always been just that. Maybe that's a big reason that the team has done so well.

If I was younger and didn't have all the experience, I might have let go, but I'd fought adversity before. I've come through bad periods and made it back to what I consider a pretty lofty position. Sure I was in a pressure cooker situation with everyone thinking I should retire, should act gracefully.

Now, it was simply on my shoulders to prove that I acted correctly. If you look at the teams in the NBA standings, you'll find the better teams are the older, more experienced ones. It makes sense. They've been through these wars before and they know how to cope with them. My situation wasn't much different.

Basically, what I am saying is that the more you've been exposed to certain situations the better you'll be able to handle them. I just knew I could conquer my problems. It's like an older team, cooler under pressure, winning on pure savvy.

In everyday life it's the same, the older one gets, the better one is able to relate to situations in the past and the more effective one will be in the future.

I liken it to the situation pilots face. Those boys fly every day. To me it's still a phenomenon, but to them it's second nature. It's like the average guy going out and hopping into his car. Flying may look difficult to the novice, but after years of concentrated effort, the job appears simple.

All that's really necessary is that you pay the price. Some people are willing to do so and others are not. That's where I am really blessed.

I used to sit and ponder for hours how the lights and shadows in our lives are in a constant state of flux. I was able to grasp this fundamental fact, and I think it's helped me adjust to problems throughout my life.

I remember when I was young, out in the fields picking cotton. I wanted to pick enough cotton to earn four dollars a day. Most of the time I couldn't make that much money because I just couldn't weigh-in that much cotton. Then I got to the point where I was able to take on the more strenuous job of hauling hay.

I had to work hard, but I could make five dollars a day hauling hay. I was so proud that I could work at the same job as my father, make the same amount of money he did, even overtime if I wanted. And I was always willing to pay what was necessary.

Of course, I received plenty of encouragement from my mother and father. They didn't particularly care what I chose for a career, but they wanted me to be a good human being. If that meant hauling hay . . . well, it was no disgrace.

They taught me to be a good Christian, to work hard and give my boss an honest day on the job, and to attend church and listen to the Lord.

I think my childhood differed to a great degree from that of the other boys in the community. When I was in high school my father still demanded that I be home at nine-thirty, unless we had a football or basketball game. He didn't allow me to drive a car until I went to college.

Naturally, people back home didn't have all the advantages of kids today. Most of them had large families and just enough to eat from day-to-day. Most of the material things were denied us, and I made up my mind that one way or the other I would attend college and make my parents proud.

Basketball was the only way in which I was going to further my education. My father didn't earn enough to be able to send me to the university. But I made it.

When I got to Grambling, one of the first things the coach said to me was that he was sure I could make it in professional basketball, but there could be no guarantee. Coach Fred Hobdy stressed the importance of an education, and after all, that's why I was at Grambling. It impressed me tremendously to know that my coach was thinking of me in much more human terms than just another basketball freak.

Other schools offered me a good chunk of money to enroll. And all I ever received at Grambling was a full athletic scholarship and ten dollars a month for laundry. But I was satisfied. I knew I was playing for the right man. And through the years, Coach Hobdy has really been an inspiration to me.

Through the years, Grambling coach Fred Hobdy has really been an inspiration to me.

All of these pictures were running through my mind when I figured I was at the crossroads. I thought of many people —for example, Lendon Stone, my high school coach and all the time he'd spent with me. I had to keep asking myself what would he expect of me in this situation.

Granted, Coach Stone was not a top NBA performer, but he is the man who took me in when I was thirteen . . . he checked to make sure I was really six-foot-five and wore a size thirteen shoe. He spent hours with me working on shooting, rebounding, and finesse on the basketball floor. We'd always stay after team practice for an hour or two, and he'd try to instill the proper perspective of sportsmanship in me.

I think Lendon Stone, more than any other individual, helped mold my values. Kids are not inherently good or bad. They are like sheep. They are there to be led, and if they are as lucky as I, they'll go along what I consider the proper path. They will not go astray. Yes, I would say that Coach Stone was a dominant force in my life . . . and more than just athletics.

Obviously, I was a big kid. I remember one time trying to protest an official's call. I stomped my foot a few times for emphasis and made a few gestures, and before I knew it Coach Stone was off the bench, hauling me from the court.

Very calmly he said, "You're finished for the night. Go to the dressing room. Until you can act like a gentleman and an athlete, you won't wear this uniform."

I knew he was right. Even then, I realized I was wrong. Apparently, he had to embarrass me to get the point across but I learned. I won't quickly forget the time I was dunking the ball while playing in the dirt schoolyard courts—we didn't have an indoor gymnasium—and Coach Stone came along. He insisted that I was just a big oaf, that I couldn't hold the basketball correctly, nor could I catch it.

A direct insult? Not really. It made me work and practice to prove to him that I was more than a big showoff, that I could and would learn the finer points of the game. And most important, that I would be more considerate of the people around me.

So while the pain lingered, I thought of Lendon Stone, Coach Hobdy at Grambling and Duke Fields, his assistant, and I tried to put them in my place. What would they do? Would they have consented to another operation, just forego the remainder of a career, take up coaching? In most

I thought time and time again of that great victory we scored against the Lakers in the 1969–70 season.

28

Sitting on the bench, I tried to spot some flaws in the other team's game. I had to keep believing I was able to contribute something. After a good win, we'd have a rehash in the team's offices.

cases, it's hard to answer for someone else, but I think I know these people, and I believe each of them would have made the same decision which I ultimately made.

Coach Fields was a very interesting person. He used to call me Bill all the time. He'd say, "Bill, you know there's no harm in falling. You just pick yourself up and get back into the race. You run a little harder than the next guy, and nobody will ever know you fell."

It was this kind of simple philosophy upon which I was raised. Coach Fields always told me to go for the moon. "If you don't get the moon, you'll definitely get a star," he used to say.

It was because of people such as these and my elementary school teachers, and others who worked with me during my formative years—Miss Velma Rogers, who led the church youth group, Misses Earline Nute, Elnora Hildreth and Annie Wilson, who taught me in the first, third and fifth grades respectively . . . these are people I can't let down.

They are the type of human beings you never want to know about any wrongdoing on your part. They have always had complete confidence in me. They've been self-sacrificing, working in the Louisiana school system for years. And they bring a whole lot more than their lunch to their jobs. They have all meant a lot to me.

As I kept thinking about them and what they would do in my situation, my problem seemed to be solved. It was now almost a rhetorical question. I don't believe any of them would think twice about giving the go-ahead sign. I don't think they would waver for an instant about the feasibility of my returning to the heights of my profession. You never pay back people because there is no way that you can.

But you try.

Now the pain was really getting to me. To try to be an important cog in the stretch run for a championship would have been like a one-legged man trying to help an old lady across the street. Neither would make it.

The decision to undergo a rehabilitation program, and the ramifications of that choice had to be quite personal. I don't consider the program a complete success even now, because the 1972–73 season was kind of an up-and-down year.

31

During the 1971–72 season, while I sat on the bench and watched my teammates go on to victory after victory, in my heart I yearned to be playing with them.

When I think of great basketball players, I always think first of Bill Russell. He was my idol.

There were stretches when I felt fine, and I could move and let loose with all the firepower I had. Yet, there were times I had to play with a somewhat guarded outlook. Before I really became involved in this extensive schedule of workouts, I had many emotional battles with myself. If I was even going to consider getting back into shape, there would be a few things in my life which would have to change. I would have to learn to accept my comeback try for just what it was. If it didn't work out, or prove viable, well, I'd have to learn to live with that also.

Sitting on the bench and watching the guys you've been playing with make the run without you has a way of making you vulnerable for what seems like endless waves of depression. Still, I knew that if I was to rebound from this injury, that for the time being I'd have to take a back seat.

It's all emotion. Actually, basketball is all emotion for a good part of your career.

I think ballplayers who are sensitive are generally the better players. Take guys like Bill Russell who was my idol. He'd walk into the locker room and be so uptight that he'd vomit.

I've never really done that, but many a night I've been unable to fall asleep because I'm so wrapped up in the game. The tension and the pressure affect the players differently.

Clyde (Walt Frazier) plays it cool all the time, but he's really one of the most emotional men in the game today. He may not outwardly express it, but the nuances, the small things he does during a tough contest, they're recognizable, and he uses this emotion to his benefit. He always plays best under pressure.

Although my situation called for me to be level-headed and logical, it may be better that I was caught up in the emotions of the team. It was a release, an outlet, and that's something I needed desperately.

I kept thinking . . . I'm going to make it back. I know it. I can't doubt myself but I was also realistic. The pain I felt was like a Chinese torture test. And each day when I thought I should feel a little better, it stayed the same.

This battle, it dawned on me, was far more difficult than facing a Wilt Chamberlain or a Kareem Abdul-Jabbar. And I didn't have anybody to help me. If I was going to make a comeback, it was completely up to Willis Reed.

It was time to see what I was made of.

The Rehabilitation Program

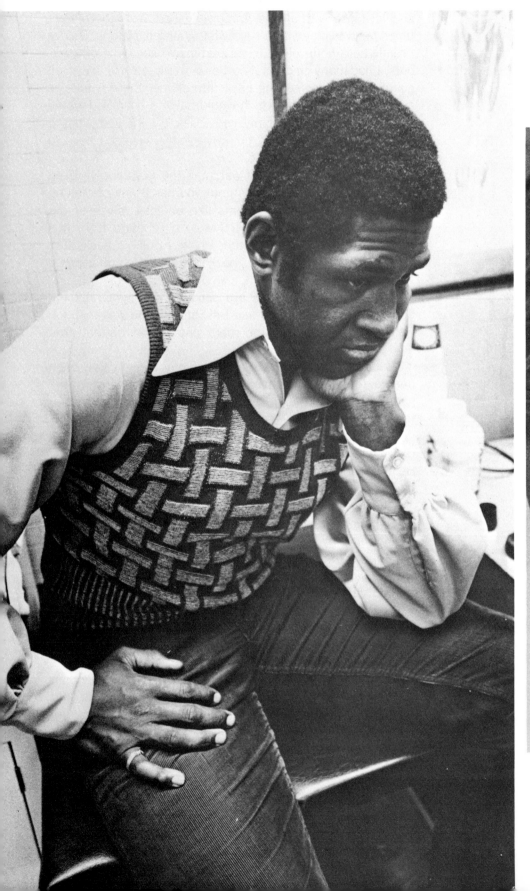

At times I was very depressed but there was never any doubt that I would proceed with Dr. Patterson (above) and Dr. O'Donohue's rehabilitation program.

In college, it's fun to play basketball. You're out there on the weekends and you're winning and having a good time. In the pros you're liable to have three games on three consecutive nights in three different towns, and you may be in California one night, Atlanta the next, and New York or Philadelphia the third. It's a business and some nights you have to play when your ankle hurts or your shoulder muscles are torn. Yet here I was, wishing I could play no matter what my condition.

Dave DeBusschere has what sounds like a simple philosophy, but is in actuality very deep. He says, "Well, you've got to play, you might as well win it." I think that's rather complex, because what Dave's trying to get across is that it takes the same amount of effort to lose a fight as to win it. And that's just what I was going to have to do—win. There was no way I was going to let this injury get the better of me.

I had had losses and hardships before and they had reinforced my belief. One should always try to do better the next time. It gives you a greater desire and determination to meet the next crisis.

Once the initial shock of the injury was over, there was never any doubt that I would proceed with the rehabilitation program suggested by the team physician, Dr. Andrew Patterson, and Dr. O'Donohue, who is considered one of the foremost authorities on tendonitis in the country.

Both Dr. Donald O'Donohue and Dr. Patterson said a rehabilitation program could put me back on my feet and onto the basketball floor. They are top men in their profession. I had no reason to doubt them. I think they had as great a desire to win as I did. Sometimes I felt they were going through the spasms with me. They were very kind and patient. I couldn't have picked better teammates.

When I think about it, there just was no alternative. I had to keep playing, continue pushing myself, proving myself.

Basketball was my life. I had other offers—in basketball and out—but basically, I am a player, a man who enjoys going out there and batting heads for forty-eight minutes a game, 100 times a year. I didn't want to coach, or go into broadcasting as so many of yesterday's sports stars have done. It's like a one-way street, and when you drive down and you are headed in the right direction, you don't suddenly make a U-turn.

I had to play . . . no matter the cost.

Still, my whole life took on a new dimension with the injury, and its repercussions. Although I knew I had to get back out there with Red Holzman and the rest of the team, I was vague as to my ability to do so. I just kept dwelling on the negatives, it seems. What if I was never able to play again?

These are more than rhetorical questions, but the answers lurk only in the shadows of your mind, because your innermost feelings keep telling you, "Willis, you have to play again. Willis, you will play. Willis, just be patient . . . the team needs you."

Just when you think you've convinced yourself, once again deep-seated doubt rises to the surface. Everything becomes murky. There's a double-edged answer. You begin to look for hidden meanings in a conversation . . . an inflection . . . a gesture . . . a word or two irresponsibly dropped takes on such significance.

Some days I felt well enough to go out there and stand up with anyone, even on the court. I felt I could go full steam. My knee didn't bother me . . . my spirits were lifted. I was once again at peace with the world.

But this feeling could be very deceiving because the next morning I might wake up and the pain would be shooting up and down my leg. I would have a difficult time just getting out of bed and making some coffee.

This constant pendulum-like situation only contributed to the aggravation and unrest. I never knew what to expect, or for that matter, how I would react.

The more I kept thinking about it, the worse it seemed. I could weave myself into such states of depression, such "pits" that I never before knew existed. It was the reverse of what I had been doing all my life . . . psyching myself up for the big games.

I'd like to be able to think that I always started out the day with the same "high," but there is no sense kidding myself. Doubt and fear played a great role . . . probably the two principal factors motivating my recovery.

I began to lose interest in a great many things around me and became more withdrawn. I know that some of the people around Madison Square Garden and the reporters might have thought it unusual for me but my emotions were mixed up. Everything seemed cloudy. I found it hard to be the same happy-go-lucky Willis Reed who had come to New York in 1964 and played seven years for the Knicks. If I

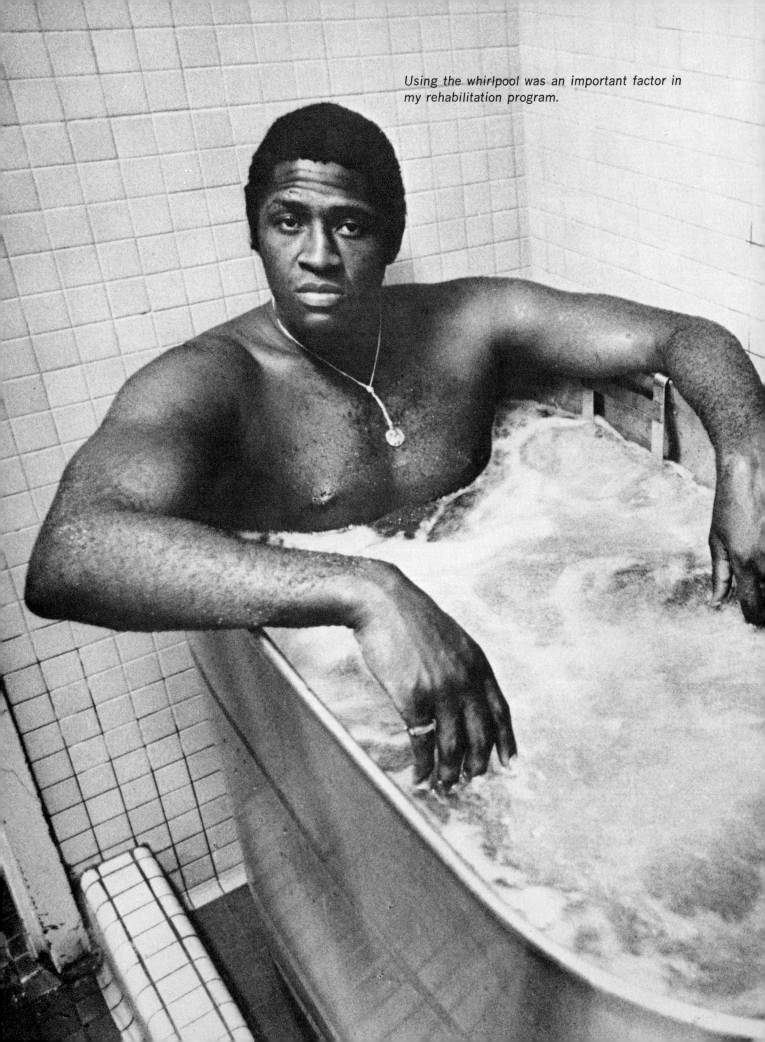

Using the whirlpool was an important factor in my rehabilitation program.

turned off some people I can understand it, but I would like to say I am sorry, and I hope they understand the circumstances.

If I could have bought a smile at Macys or Gimbels or in a supermarket, I certainly would have. But I just couldn't force myself to be jolly. I had to take time, get away and rest.

Of course, the first thing would be to adhere to the doctors' instructions. This wasn't as easy as it sounds. When Dr. O'Donohue was consulted and later brought in on the case, he was fairly certain there was no real physical damage to my knee.

I began wondering if it could all be mental. I knew what I felt, and it was excruciating. So I listened to Dr. O'Donohue and finally decided: "Well, this man's the boss. He knows his business a heckuva lot better than I do. I'll just have to go along with him . . . at least for awhile."

The first thing Dr. O'Donohue did was to put a walking cast on my leg. He said he saw no tear of the muscle or tendon, not even an inflammation . . . although I had been through a bout with the latter earlier in the year.

He told me not to put any undue stress on my leg. That meant no running, and walking as little as possible. I couldn't even stand the pain when I sat normally with my knees bent. The good doctor explained that when I sat I would have to force myself to keep my leg straight out, flexing the muscles as little as possible.

All those days of agony. I kept remembering my last moments on the court, those futile gestures. I had played about ten minutes against the Warriors . . . didn't score . . . couldn't move . . . and managed only five rebounds.

I had walked off the court at halftime; and in my heart I knew it would be quite a while before I returned . . . just how long I'd have to wait and see. I got dressed while the team started the second half. We looked unprofessional out there, and I kept saying to myself, "Don't worry, guys, I'll be back. I'll return and when I do we'll wipe up this league. We'll take home another crown for the Knicks."

But there was nothing I could do about it until my knee came around. It was time to leave the team . . . let them pick up a few pieces . . . go away and think. I decided I'd go back home and do some fishing.

For the next six weeks I retreated from the land of fuss and frolic—New York City. I caught some good size catfish, and went shrimping a few times. I thought it would be a form of therapy, the relaxation.

One of my first encounters with Wilt Chamberlain, when he was playing for the Philadelphia Warriors. In those years, Wilt was the dominating offensive force in the NBA.

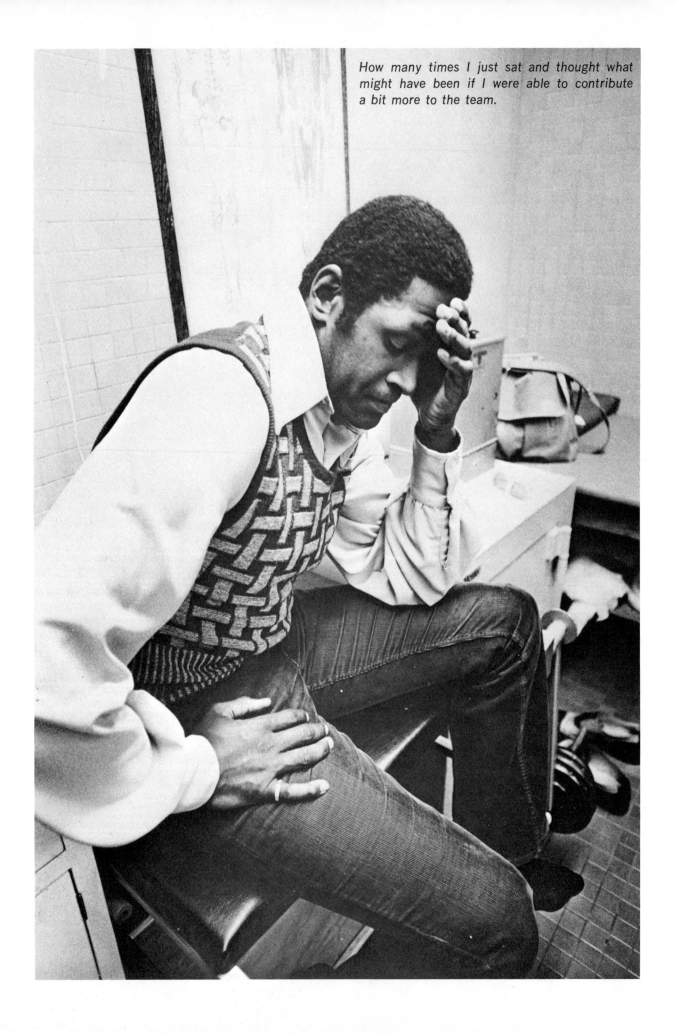

How many times I just sat and thought what might have been if I were able to contribute a bit more to the team.

It was impossible. I was so keyed up and worried, I never enjoyed a fishing trip less. It was like an enforced vacation . . . there is no such thing. Sure, I was in the Bayou country rather than Manhattan, but the same thoughts kept creeping back. If there's nothing physically wrong with me, why am I in such agony? Will I ever be able to play again? Am I over the hill at twenty-nine?

Did you ever sit home and watch the soap operas on television? Man, I thought that I'd go batty with "As the World Turns" and "The Edge of Night." The characters in these series have more mental hangups than a centipede has legs.

So fishing and relaxing turned out to be a flop . . . not because I didn't catch my share of fish, but because I just couldn't run away from my problems. Maybe Thoreau was able to run away from the city life . . . then again, he didn't play center for the New York Knicks. The city had become a part of me.

I had a good many friends there and I didn't realize how much I'd miss the life. I couldn't walk backward down to Louisiana. I worked hard to get out of there, and the pain was just as unbearable in the South as it was in New York.

As a matter of fact I continued to have the feeling of a man in a science fiction flick—the one who is suspended in space, unaware of his surroundings or the gravitational pulls around him. He wonders if he'll ever see land again. If he'll ever be like other people after having experienced something so incomprehensible.

And believe me, there is no one thing so incomprehensible as pain, especially when it is explained that there is no pathological reason for it.

After I came back to New York, Dr. O'Donohue was ready to start his program. What I thought was going to be whirlpool and ice baths, and rubdowns, turned out to be little more than a program involving weights on my legs. Dr. O'Donohue had charted four types of exercises for the area, all involving these weights.

It was so simple that one might say it was sophisticated. He called these exercises a back lift, two side lifts, and a front lift.

Can you believe that the most up-to-date remedy for a case of tendonitis is the lifting of a few weights? I just didn't think that I was going to be able to work myself back into shape like that. But I had promised to give it a try. And I did.

I had faith in Dr. O'Donohue. I traveled back and forth to Oklahoma City on a regular basis to see him. If he was wrong, I was really in trouble. He explained that the intensity of the program would increase, and told me that even though there might be no outward signs of progress for a good period of time, the healing process would be going on.

Obviously, he couldn't give me any guarantees. And I don't think I would have liked any, since I knew the entire situation to be unpredictable. If there's only one road to the farm stand, one takes it.

When I began the program on a regular basis, it was just a matter of lifting as much weight as I could with my left leg. It was all a matter of judgment . . . by that I mean if I could lift five pounds successfully then I would try seven or ten, the maximum amount I could bear without pain.

The program involved various amounts of exercises with the weights three times each day. It was as much a matter of discipline as anything else. And I still had that feeling that the pain was as debasing as it was debilitating, since pathologically I was a fine specimen.

The first week or so of active participation in the program I could hardly lift my leg . . . that was without any weights. I was soon getting discouraged, but then I spoke with Dr. O'Donohue.

He explained that although nothing was detected in the tests, he believed that after I had my knee operated on in 1970, the muscle atrophied and never quite recovered.

Dr. O'Donohue was a very patient man, because I guess I'm one of those headstrong people who has to be shown everything. It wasn't that I didn't believe in the doctor, or even the therapy, it was just that there were no immediate signs of progress.

Dr. O'Donohue explained that my right leg was far more developed than my left, and that was causing constant stress. Consequently, I was demanding too much of the left side of my body.

Everything the doc said seemed logical. I couldn't put my finger on any source, and I sure didn't want to blame the operation for my problems, especially since I'd played an entire season following surgery.

I just had to return. I had to keep working

46

The pain let up only on rare occasions. At night, I would lie in bed and wonder if things would ever return to normal. Usually I am a pretty good sleeper. But with the injury and the mental anguish, I was unable to close my eyes most of the time. I was getting less sleep than if I were on the road and this definitely didn't help my disposition.

I had made up my mind that the rehabilitation program was right for me, although many times I lay in bed questioning my decision.

Each day, I would rise early in the morning and go through my standard set of exercises. Then maybe I would lie down for a while to get off my leg, or maybe I'd run a few errands in the city. Even so, just before lunch, I would be back home doing the lifts. I'd repeat the procedure at night. I had to work my leg as hard as possible without straining it.

It had to be a matter of complete dedication and commitment. There could be no day on which I'd skip the exercises just because I didn't feel like pushing myself. It had to be a daily routine. After all, it seemed to be my only opportunity to play basketball again.

Sometimes I would watch the guys practice when they were in New York. I would try and kibbitz with them, give them the needle, and let them know I was keeping an eye on the box scores. But my heart really wasn't in it and the boys were very understanding. I wouldn't stay long. I'd manage a smile, and then leave.

I spent some time hanging around the office, talking with the Knicks' publicity director, Jim Wergeles, and the girls who were busy answering the phones and typing. Jimmy has been a great friend and confidante through the years. We had worked together on the Willis Reed summer camp and other ventures. I guess if I was going to unload to anyone it would be Jimmy.

Again however, everyone appeared cautious in their speech. I'm sure they all wanted to do the right thing and not hurt my feelings. Maybe I was just looking for a reason to become more somber. It just wasn't the old ball of laughs it had always been before the injury . . . while I was playing.

Whenever I sat down, I would have to support my leg on something. The Knicks have a nice comfortable couch in the outer office, so I'd sit there and look at my mail.

In my earliest years with the Knicks, one of my greatest assets was my ability to leap and block shots.

The fan mail was always encouraging. I guess everyone likes to get fan mail, but when I was hurt and unable to play . . . with the prospects getting dimmer, the fan mail was like a real tonic.

I was really surprised how much the people knew about the nature of my problem. I was also astounded at the empathy shown and the sympathy expressed. Once again I realized how fortunate I was to be playing in New York City.

These people seemed the most warm-hearted and concerned group I had ever encountered. They were just beautiful. The greatest fans anywhere. There were many words of wisdom in those letters, not the least of which was to remind me of next season—to have patience.

Sure, it's egotistical to a degree. But now I had the time to sit down and answer those Knick fans who had done so much to support me and the team over the years. I could give a little bit back to the game. If only I could get out of those doldrums.

The team began picking up steam as the season wore on. Lucas was playing well and it looked as though the Knicks might go all the way . . . without me. I still felt pangs of regret everytime I'd go to a contest and sit on the bench in street clothes, unable to get in there and mix it up, unable to contribute.

But Red always included me in the skull sessions and was always anxious for my opinions. He tried to make me feel I was a big boost to the team's morale, that there were many ways I could help although I wasn't wearing the uniform. I enjoyed the compliment, but it failed to shake me out of the rut of frustration. I'd only speak longingly of the day I would be able to return to the wars.

We had many a rap session on my account. Red, Dick McGuire, the reporters and myself.

We would analyze the strengths and weaknesses of all the opposing teams. We would figure out how to counteract their strong points. There were a good many personal anecdotes thrown in. Some were really funny. But in a way I was just trying to be polite. It is very hard to be involved when you are a ballplayer and not playing ball. And it was harder still to laugh.

I appreciated the job the team was doing, and although I knew I wouldn't be back in the 1971-72 season, there were ever-increasing flickers of hope for the following year.

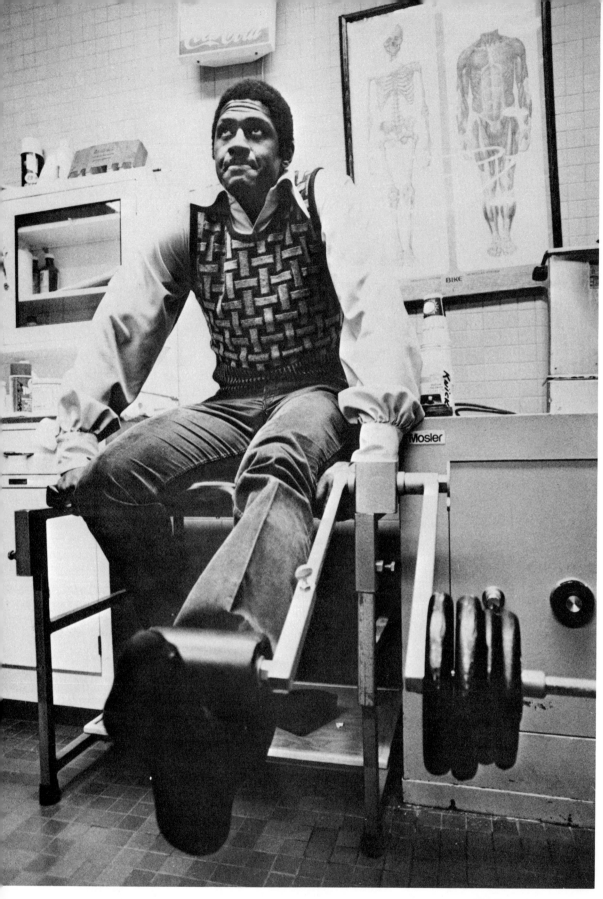

I believed completely in Dr. O'Donohue's weights program.

Positive signs were appearing more frequently now. I had established the routine and was working with greater weights than I had thought possible. There were times when the strength in my leg exceeded my wildest expectations.

There were also times when I would just get disgusted, throw my jacket on and leave the house, because I was unable to progress at the projected rate. I'd begin to think it was all a waste of time . . . how did I ever get talked into this program?

But the next day I'd be back there with the weights on my legs going through all the same contortions, both mentally and physically. In a way I guess I knew my leg was responding, getting stronger, but it was tough to admit as long as I was confined to a year of not playing, a season of doubt.

I also felt I wasn't earning my money. I wasn't helping anyone. That's one of the worst feelings in the world. People have to be needed, they want to be used.

Although I had played only eleven games when I had to rest for the remainder of the season, it was undoubtedly the longest campaign of my life.

I replayed almost every moment of every game in which I had ever participated—high school, college, and with the Knicks. I remembered the good shots, the happiness of winning and I also saw all the mistakes I had made on the court and I kept thinking what a nebulous art hindsight can be when there was nothing you could do to change the situation.

Every pivotal play—indelible in my memory. How I would handle certain players and situations. The season just dragged. I would rather have played 300 games that year . . . forty-eight minutes every contest. It would have been a heck of a lot less arduous. I kept thinking I was losing the war of nerves.

Granted, I was getting out more now, seeing a lot more of the games. The Knicks had started winning and were picking up steam coming into the stretch, but we still lacked the big man who could block out and take charge.

Walt Frazier had taken on the leadership of the team and was carrying it off well. Of course, DeBusschere is always the inspiration. Things were coming along better for the team. Looking back, I could say things were beginning to break for me too.

53

There was no sudden surge of strength in my left leg, but a gradual feeling of muscle tension and relaxation. To pinpoint one day and say this was when I really knew I was going to be all right would be ridiculous.

That is not to say there were no encouraging signs. The exercises had given me confidence in the ability of my leg to respond. I could sit now without having to raise my leg. I was able to walk without pain more frequently. The entire situation was becoming progressively more endurable.

It was a long time before I could actually smile, but as the pain began to subside, I did. I still didn't know definitely if I would ever play basketball again until I tried to run and jump and pivot . . . and I also knew it would be a good nine months before I could put any stress on my knee.

By the time the playoffs rolled around I felt my knee was almost completely healed but I was far from being in condition. I didn't have any wind. I hadn't run in five months. I was a bit overweight. I would be of no help . . . not that year.

As everyone knows we managed to defeat the Baltimore Bullets and the Boston Celtics for a spot in the National Basketball Association playoff finals. But the Los Angeles Lakers did us in, and I wondered if I had been able to play, perhaps the team would have won the flag.

Wilt Chamberlain had a great series against us. He played with the vigor of a nineteen-year-old college sophomore. And we had nobody to contain him. Although Wilt's figures don't show impressively in the scoring column, he was the man who beat us. He played top-drawer defense, blocking a good many of our shots and intimidating our smaller forwards and guards.

Wilt also blocked out Luke and DeBusschere effectively both on the offensive and defensive boards. Jerry West, Gail Goodrich and Jim McMillian were using Wilt as a big post, cutting off him, getting the screened shots.

Ours was a futile effort. With Chamberlain getting the out pass, even their running game was clicking. The Lakers looked like a powerhouse . . . and there was no denying them.

However, I have always had pretty good luck against Wilt. I have the brawn to battle him for the rebounds as well as the ability to go outside for the jumper. Nobody can say they have consistently outplayed Chamberlain. Wilt's too strong and too smart a player.

I love to work with kids, watch them mature physically and mentally. Kids are the heart of basketball.

It hurt me to see the team faced with the difficult task of stopping Chamberlain, and I tried to help Lucas and DeBusschere with advice on how I had played him in the past.

I was becoming more certain now that I'd play against Wilt again. The question had changed from would I ever play again to would I play another season without pain. I was reasonably certain that the following August I would be wearing the Knick uniform.

The year I had just spent had been the most grueling, unsatisfying chunk of time in my life. I had scratched for answers, come up empty and doubting. I became suspicious and worried and fearful. I had lost and then regained that quality which is so dear to me—pride.

I had also developed a new sense of self-respect, and was more able to cope. But the day-to-day barometer of emotion had been cracked. I was on a sliding scale for a year, completely unknown, as if I had lived in a vacuum.

After the playoffs I went about my business as usual, except that I didn't go hunting. For the first time that I could remember I didn't take to the trail with my gun. I was determined to rest as much as possible since I was continuing the exercise program, and was consulting the doctor regularly.

At the Willis Reed summer camp, I put on my gym clothes and went out to help the youngsters. It felt as if I were standing on two poles. I was still stiff and unaccustomed to fluid movement.

I began running, determined to work back into shape. My leg no longer gave me problems. There was no unexpected pain. Soon I was on the basketball courts with the kids. Naturally, I wasn't going 100 percent, but I was there again. I was playing that big ole grand, lovable game that Dr. Naismith invented.

Each day I moved a little better, stayed on the court a bit longer. Then I started playing one-on-one against some of the instructors, NBA players. And I was reasonably satisfied with my physical state.

I kept needling my good friend, Bob Lanier, of the Detroit Pistons, into playing against me. He's a darned good basketball player, and I wanted the feeling of being matched against the rough center. Any reticence I had was gone.

After I had reached the point where I was considered to be in good enough condition to play again, I was told by the doctors that I would have to wear a knee brace whenever I played.

At my All-Star camp the feel of the ball was almost foreign to me but I ran a bit, shot some baskets, and made my own decision as to when I had worked out enough.

The first day back, the first scrimmage, the first complete test . . . you'd think that Jerry Lucas would take it easy on me. Never.

I reported to camp at Monmouth College at West Long Branch, New Jersey, and it seemed like the big question on everyone's mind was whether Willis would be able to bounce back or not.

I felt confident.

Still, I hadn't put myself to the real test. I knew the questions were not going to be answered the first day or even the first few weeks of training and so did Coach Red Holzman.

He was just great about it, allowing me to set my own pace, work in with the team gradually. He told me to make my own timetable, just let him know when I was ready.

Red tries to give one the impression that he's a hard, tough, impersonal coach. He's really just a pussycat with more knowledge of basketball than any man I've ever known. He's a warm, sensitive man. And every time I told him I was ready to participate a little more, Red would say, ''Make sure, Willis; if it bothers you just come right out.''

The press, actually everyone following the team, knew we were in need of a ''big center;'' somebody who could get in there and trade with the likes of Chamberlain, Abdul-Jabbar, Thurmond and Lanier. If we were to win, we'd have to have someone who could block up the middle.

Jerry Lucas had done a great job the previous year while I was trying to recuperate, but he's a natural forward, a tremendous player in his own right. He's six-foot-eight and has the shooting touch and range of a much smaller man.

Luke, however, doesn't have the brawn to battle with the big guys under the boards. And we were in need of someone who could go in there and rebound, as well as shut off the lanes on defense. A big part of my job is to set up the picks for guys like Clyde and Earl, even for Bill Bradley and DeBusschere. That way we try and free a man for an easier shot.

When Lucas is at center and we don't have the muscle to screen out the area, we're forced to change our game. Luke tries to draw his man outside with the threat of his long bombs, and allows DeBusschere to do a good share of the rebounding.

Jerry has also been plagued by knee problems and is forced to put ice packs on them after every contest. Hopefully, between the two of us, we'd come up with at least one healthy center.

I guess I never quite realized how difficult it was to touch my toes.

Luke and Earl had a year working under our system, and it is tough to adapt. We looked like we were in the enviable situation of having All-Stars at every position. Clyde and Earl in the backcourt, Dave and Luke as forwards and Willis Reed at center, not to mention Bill Bradley who has done a lot to help make our team a winner.

It appeared as if all we had to do was show up and the other teams would fall over. But this is never the case in a league like the NBA. And we were going to have to work and work hard.

When we started the exhibition games, Earl was still bothered by bone spurs, Jerry's knees were acting up and I was a bit slow responding. So the Knicks with all their superstars took good long looks at some of the rookies.

Although they were only exhibitions, the team was showing signs of inconsistency . . . we'd get hot and run the opposition off the floor one period, then we'd die. There's no question that on paper we had the personnel to go all the way. But again, they make you play eighty-two games during the season just to prove it.

Our camp is not as tightly run as some of the others in the NBA. That's because most of us have been around for a number of years and we know best how to clock ourselves. It's the rookies and second-year men who are under the gun most of the time.

This is not to excuse the way we looked in preseason. After all, that's what training camp is all about. We were ragged and most of the time we couldn't put the same five starters on the floor from one night to another. Small injuries kept cropping up—muscle pulls, bruises, hamstrings, groins. You name it, we had it. Our trainer Danny Whelan was more active than a revolving door.

Still, it was no surprise to me that we were selected by most of the local writers to win the Eastern Division. Even as we neared the tail end of the preseason, we didn't have that close-knit defense, that team defense with which Red's been able to work wonders. The offense wasn't startling, either . . . rough at best.

I kept increasing my work load, but was a long way from the Willis Reed of 1969–70 or '70–'71. And I knew it.

Knick fans are the greatest. They followed the exhibitions with a passion, always finding one reason or another why we didn't produce. Their attitude and philosophy came down to the simple, "Wait 'til the season starts."

After the season started, I spent the first five games sitting on the bench.

But we got off on the wrong foot, still looking sluggish and inconsistent. We continued to be unable to work with the same men. This was truly a team effort. From one night to another, nobody knew who was going to show up lame.

As a result, swing men like Phil Jackson and Luke got in a lot of time, both at forward and center. John Gianelli, a rookie with plenty of aggressiveness, was also taking his turn in the pivot. I was far from ready to go forty-eight minutes. I was still having a tough time moving, and feeling awkward after the layoff.

With each game, however, I was feeling stronger. I had better muscle tone and greater endurance. My timing was beginning to click.

The press continued to demand that the Knicks trade for an established center. A few writers wrote me off after seeing my early-season performances. The guys on the team, however, remained as encouraging as ever.

I was holding back a little, maybe. I had to work myself into condition. Although I trained as hard as ever, possibly it wasn't enough. These thoughts kept running through my mind. I kept wondering when I'd be able to answer my critics.

Most important, the team had not jelled yet. Was it just a matter of time? I thought that to be the case.

As slow as we were in getting started, that's how fast Boston came out of the gate. A lot of people spurned the Celtics in the preseason polls, but they are a tough team . . . especially in Boston Garden.

Earl was playing a little more now and Dick Barnett was in there with Clyde most of the time in the backcourt. Dean Meminger, my roommate, was really beginning to come through with some clutch performances. With Deano and Clyde playing at the same time, it's almost a good bet the opposition won't cross mid-court. Man, what hands those guys have, and they are quicker than a pair of Siamese cats.

Of course, Red wasn't satisfied with the progress of the team. The only starters he could depend on for a while were Bradley, Dave and Clyde. But Jackson was getting better all the time, as was Gianelli. Henry Bibby added strength to the backcourt, although it was only his rookie season.

We were not a five-man team, nor even an eight-man squad as many have made out to be the case. We were and are a twelve-man ball club, and everyone earns his salary. I can't stress that too much.

Even Ned Irish (background) came to practice on Oct. 20th. That was the day I told Red I was available for duty.

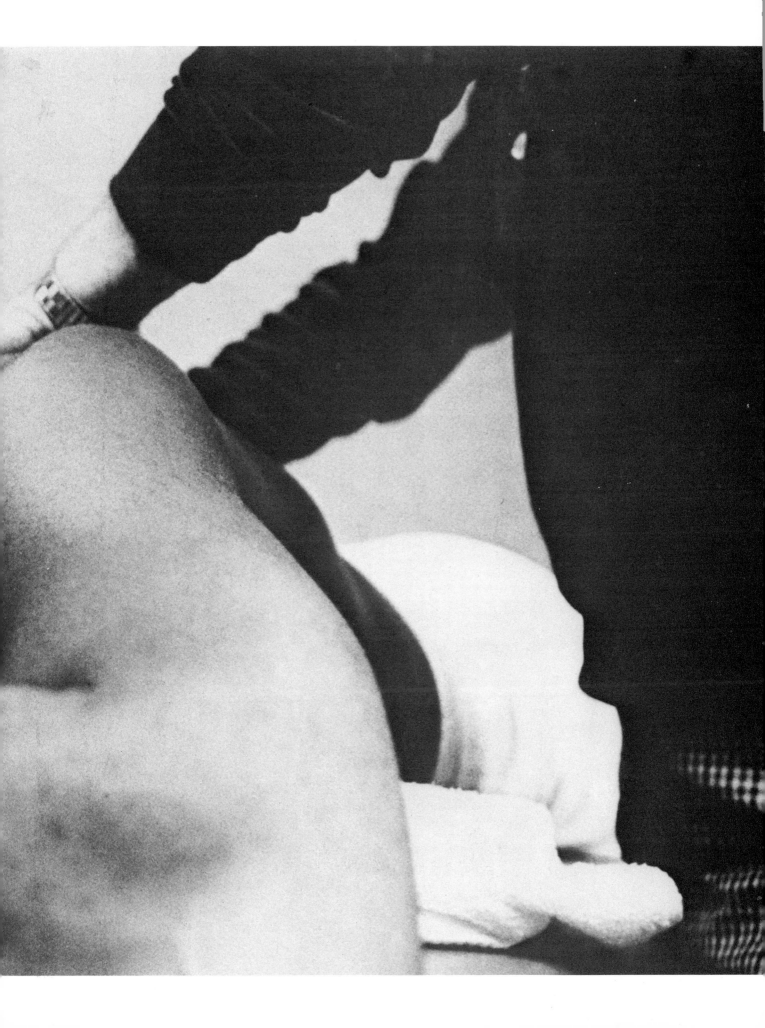

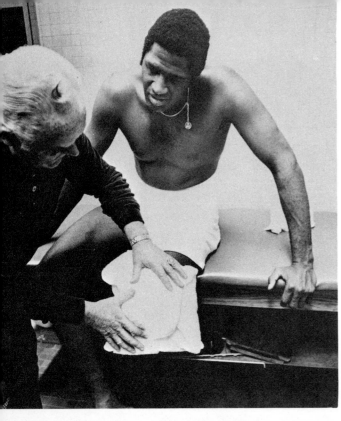

After trying four braces, I found one that was comfortable.

Trainer Danny Whelan was invaluable throughout my rehabilitation months.

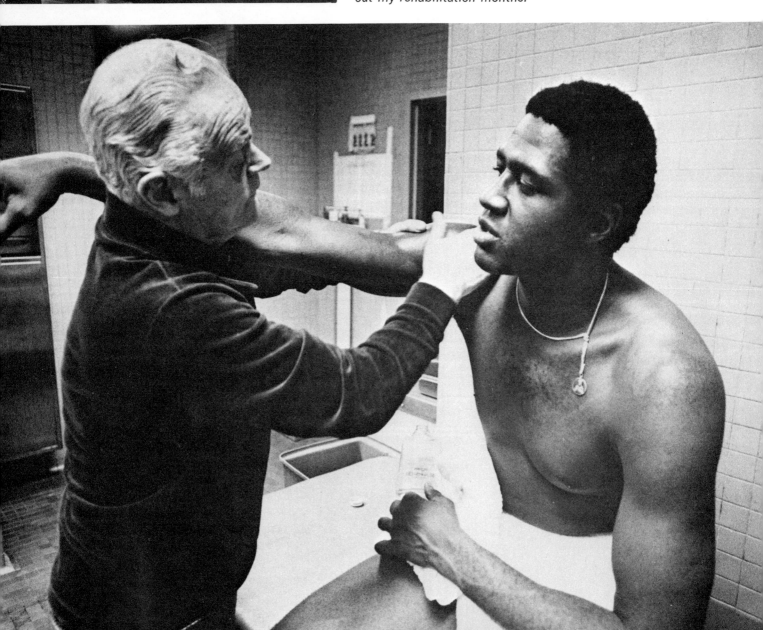

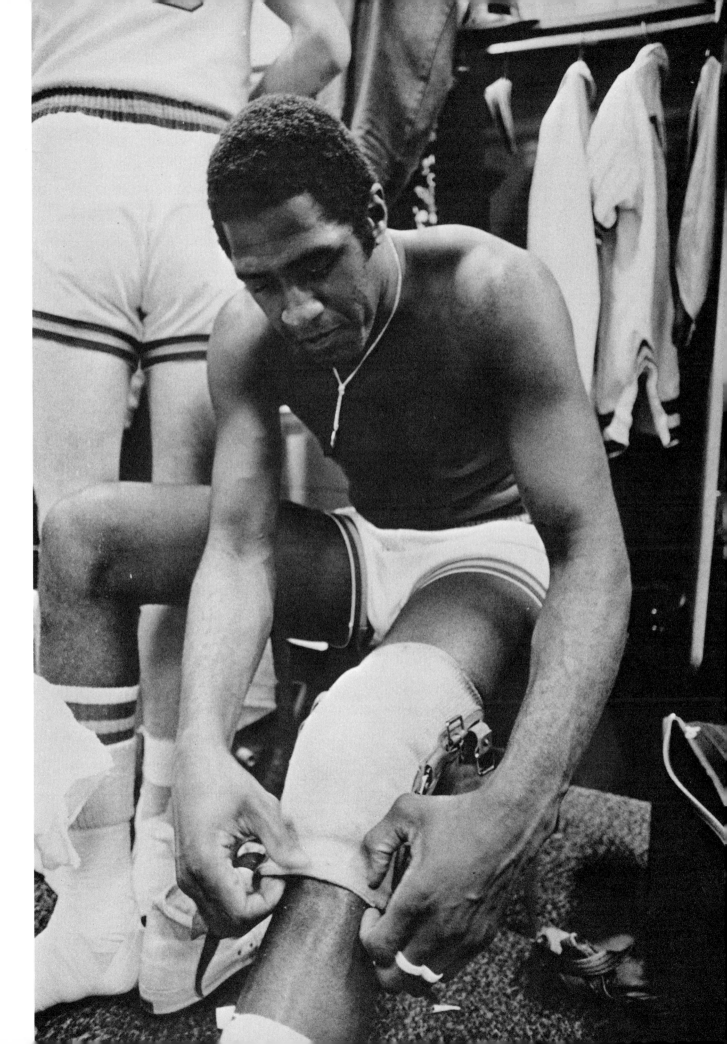

I was touched by the fans' devotion as they gave me a three minute standing ovation before my first regular season game in almost a year. It was against the Philadelphia 76ers.

Cutting and moving on the fast break were still the weakest parts of my game.

All right, so we were going along somewhat like a boat on troubled waters. We'd look good one game, bad the next. Then we'd have a mediocre showing, good enough to lead the fans into believing again. But the best that could be said for that early season form was that we were adequate . . . nothing more.

Red and Dick McGuire, our head scout, put in many a sleepless night trying to figure out that enigma.

I don't think I was hurting the team as much as some of the newspaper accounts stated. I wasn't a big help though and I certainly wasn't content with the way I was performing.

The healthier we got the more we began to pour it on. We had some good luck against the front runners. Head-to-head we were beating Boston, Milwaukee and Los Angeles. But then we'd get beaten by Chicago or Phoenix or Golden State. There is no time for a breather in the league since you never can tell what will happen next.

The Celtics, meanwhile, were building up an insurmountable lead in the Eastern Division. They would use their running game and clean up against the lesser lights. The only team, I'd say, that didn't pose a potential threat was the Philadelphia 76ers. But Baltimore, Boston or the Knicks were capable of running off a streak to take over the lead in the East.

The Bullets are a good deal tougher than most observers would let you believe. Since getting Archie Clark and Elvin Hayes in trades, they've got scoring power. They always had the tough rebounding of Wes Unseld . . . he's truly one of the great players in the NBA. One of the big things that was hurting the Bullets was the absence of veteran Gus Johnson, a top scorer and rebounder of the previous year.

They had picked up Mike Riordan and Dave Stallworth from us in the Monroe deal, and Riordan was surprising quite a few people around the league with his aggressive, hang-in-there style of play. What's more, he was coming into his own as a scorer. Yes, the Bullets were tough, and they'd be tough all year.

Gene Shue had put together a fine ball club and I think if Clark hadn't staged such an extended holdout, they would have been a lot more trouble for everyone.

The fans at Madison Square Garden kept bringing in signs like—We're No. 1 . . . Let's Go Knicks . . . Come on Willis. We were honestly doing our best.

Once in a while you just have to blow your top. This time it was Philadelphia's Dale Schlueter who was the antagonist.

76

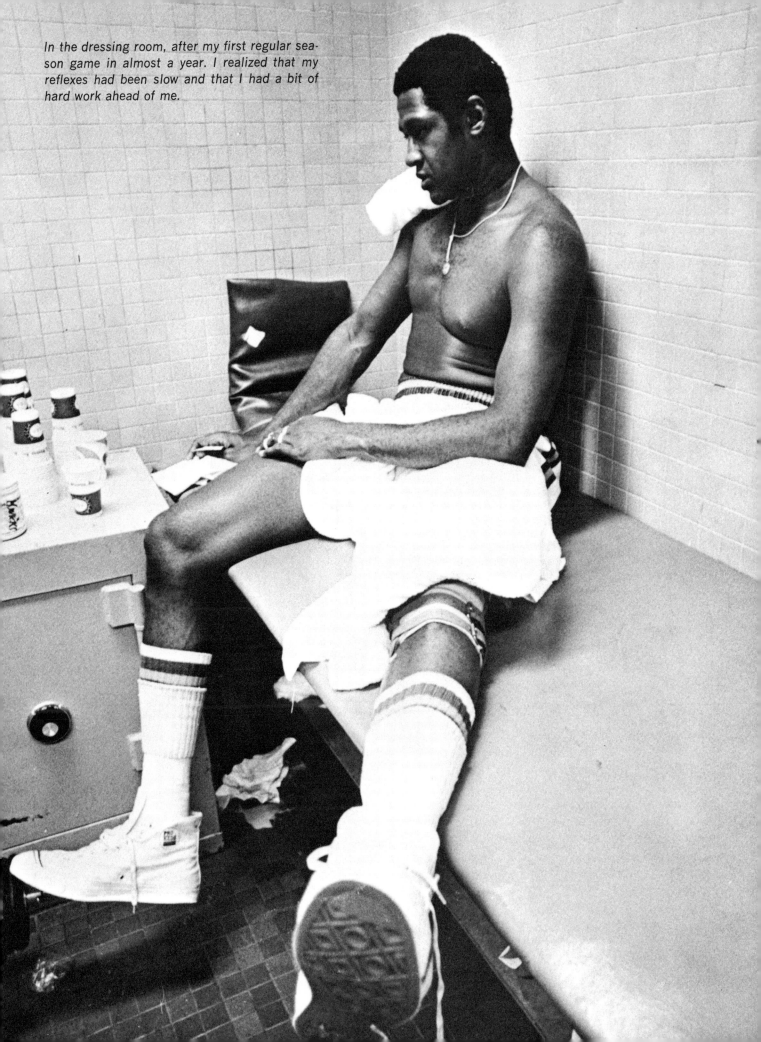

In the dressing room, after my first regular season game in almost a year. I realized that my reflexes had been slow and that I had a bit of hard work ahead of me.

We'd pore over game films for hours. The practice sessions at Pace College and in the Garden never slackened as the season went on. I think they intensified. Red was out to give New York a winner. But every night when we'd look at the box scores the Celtics would have won another.

If we were going to make a real move, it would have to be soon. I can't pick one game and say that was the turning point of our season. But there was a stretch, right after Earl was ready to play, that everyone was available—that certainly helped and was a big factor in our resurgence.

I was feeling better all the time. I may not have been the Willis Reed the fans at the Garden remembered . . . before the 1969–70 season. But there were many good moments. The doctors were enthusiastic about my progress and I felt I was contributing more to the success of the team.

Luke's knees kept him out of action for a time and then I began playing every day. Gianelli or Jackson spelled me, but I was getting just the therapy I needed at this point . . . I was in the lineup.

There was still a long way to go. I knew it. I was having trouble with my jump shot, and I had to present some kind of a scoring threat. My maneuverability was not what it should have been, but with the help of DeBusschere and Clyde I was able to get the rebounding job done.

We were becoming a steadier, more balanced club, and the defense began to mesh. It seemed as if each night someone else had the hot hand. There was no one player the opposition could double-up on. We could all score and now we were doing it.

Just as there always seemed to be another man on the injured rolls, there always appeared to be another man taking up the slack. Actually, Bradley was the only guy to play in every contest, although most of the boys would have run through a wall, had Red asked them.

DeBusschere, Frazier and Bradley made the All-Star team, and Clyde led the squad in scoring with just a shade better than twenty points per game (21.1), but it seemed as if everyone had a shining moment.

Gianelli's tough play won a pair of games for us; Bibby hit a couple of last minute baskets to give us victories; Harthorne Wingo won a few. I can't say enough about Jackson. Here was a guy, who just a couple of seasons ago, everyone had crossed off their list because of his back problems.

One thing about Red . . . he always allowed me to make the decisions as to my playing time.

Still feeling my way. My eighth game of the season, against the Atlanta Hawks, proved one of the worst for me. However, we beat the Hawks, holding them to under 100 points which was to be a defensive trend for the remainder of the season against most other teams.

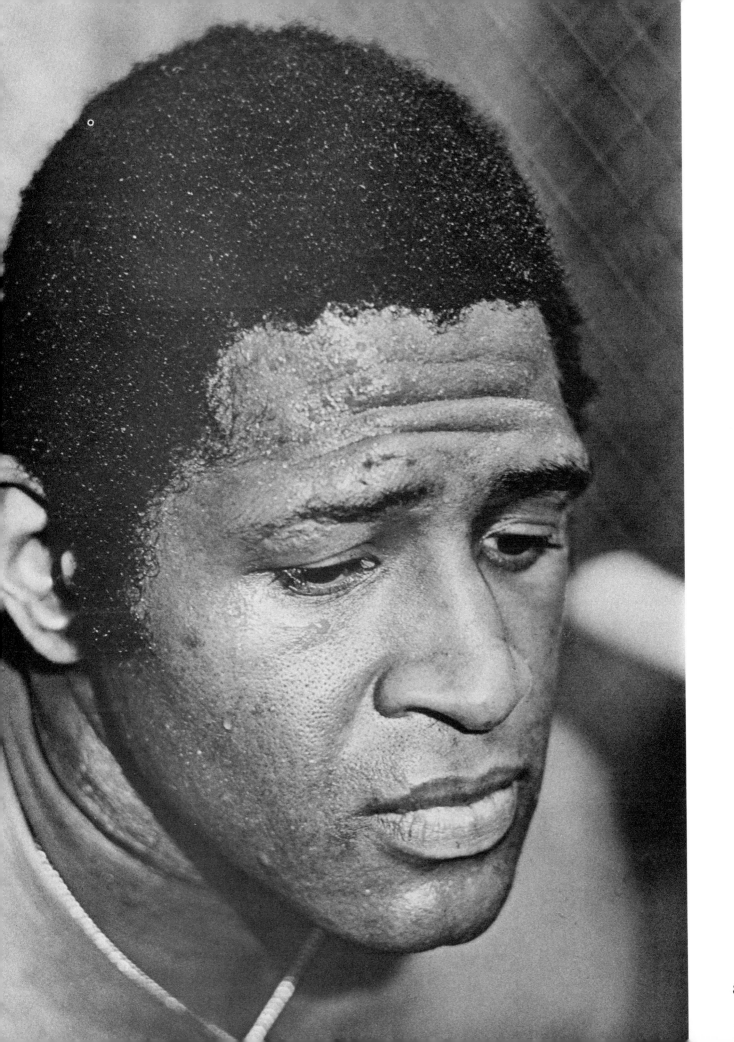

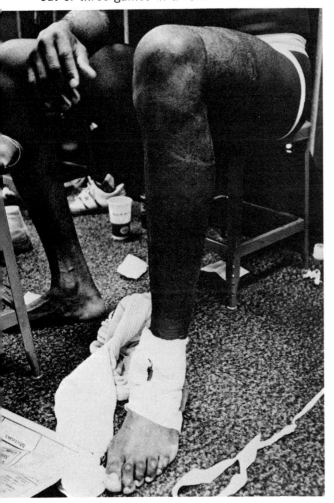

It wasn't always easy. A burn on my left foot, which I played on for awhile, finally kept me out of three games in a row.

Now, he was scoring better than ever and playing the kind of defense we needed. His timing was back and he was blocking as many shots as ever. That long arm span, combined with a new aggressiveness made him one of the most valuable players on the club, going down the stretch.

We had five guys who averaged in double figures, including myself (11.0), DeBusschere (16.3), Bradley (16.1) and Monroe (15.5). I only played in sixty-nine games, and sometimes Red just used me in spots, but I think I helped the club.

Boston was relentless. They had a bunch of young guys there—JoJo White, Don Chaney, Dave Cowens—and we didn't really believe they would be able to keep up the pace from wire to wire. Yet with the help of a few seasoned veterans like John Havlicek and Don Nelson and Paul Silas, they were the scourge of the division. Even though we did get the best of them, they won the division going away and wound up with the best won-loss record in the National Basketball Association.

Tom Heinsohn's boys had certainly proved themselves a team to be reckoned with. Milwaukee won its division as did the Lakers. The Knicks, Golden State and Baltimore, Chicago and Atlanta completed the playoff bracket.

The team defense concept Red tried to instill in the Knicks paid off for us at the end of the regular season. We knew the Celtics had the division clinched and that we would definitely be in the playoffs, so Red rested us more liberally, and the defense was able to keep all the games within reach.

As a matter of fact, if you asked me what characterizes our club more than anything else I would have to say the defense.

The fans, led by Dancing Harry, a kind of carnival-like dancer who dresses in the most outrageous of outfits, have really become a part of this squad. When you speak to players on the other clubs around the league, you realize how much they hate to face the fans and the roars and the "hexes" and the offense of the Knicks' sixth man . . . the fans.

We started preparing for the playoffs against Baltimore. I don't know if we would rather have faced the Hawks or not. We knew the Bullets were going to be tough. They didn't disappoint us.

In a December game against Chicago we were facing one of the toughest defensive teams in the league. Here, I am scoring on a hook shot, as Cliff Ray is foiled by a fake preceding the shot.

The regular season was drawing to a close and my best game, statistically, was against the Phoenix Suns. I felt confident that I was ready for the playoffs.

A relaxing moment before the playoffs with my cousin, Herbert.

Clyde and his Rolls Royce at Mayor Lindsay's party for the team. His play is as stylish as his looks.

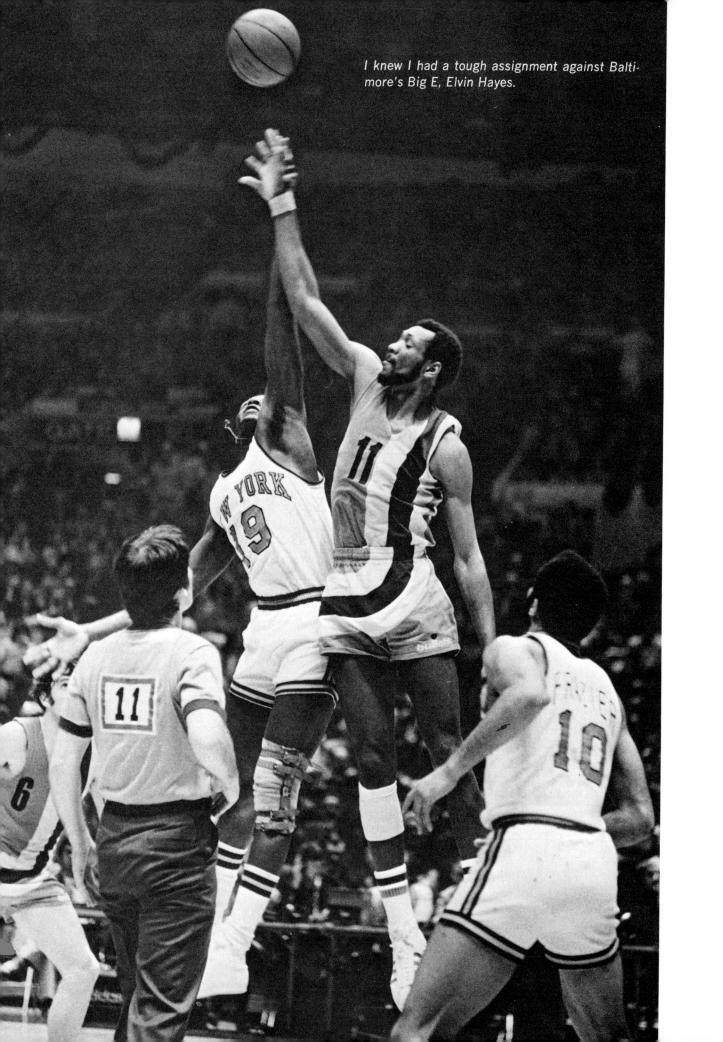

I knew I had a tough assignment against Baltimore's Big E, Elvin Hayes.

The Playoffs—
The Baltimore Bullets

The post-season games are always like starting from scratch. What you did during the year doesn't count. You have to be ready to put out 100 percent, all the time, against the toughest opposition there is. We believed we were healthy and ready to go.

The first game was played at home. It was a tough defensive struggle all the way. Neither team got 100 points, and we won, 95–83. It sounds a heckuva lot easier than it actually was. We were losing for the better part of three quarters and Baltimore unveiled a good running game with Elvin Hayes and Unseld getting their passes out quickly.

Archie Clark was penetrating well and we were just trying to play our game: set up the good shot . . . work the ball . . . hit the open man . . . play tough defense.

But the Bullets, not noted for their team play, were within reach of the gold. They were playing a strong defense as well. We were fortunate that Earl Monroe had the type of game that possibly only he is capable of playing. He looked far better than he had all season.

The playoffs bring out the best in every player and every team and Earl was able to get the feel of it. He's a natural showman anyway, but he gave the 20,000 spectators at the Garden on March 30, 1973, something truly memorable.

Earl was all over the court, playing a tough defense, stealing the ball, moving, faking, streaking for the basket, pulling up and hitting those turn-around jump shots. He was scoring from the outside, but when they would play up on him, he'd go right around them. It was something beautiful to watch.

Hayes and Unseld completely dominated the backboards, although I thought Lucas did a good job underneath. I picked off only five in my twenty-six minutes of action, but our smaller men were hustling in and stealing a few off the defensive boards. Clyde was the leading scorer with twenty-five, Dave had sixteen, and Luke fifteen. The razzle-dazzle, the showmanship, the spurts of brilliance, the crown . . . they belonged to the Earl.

Unseld and the Big E were just realizing what they could do if they concentrated on defense. I never saw Hayes block so many shots in my life before, but he had to give up something . . . managing only sixteen points. Archie Clark again was our nemesis with twenty-two points. We knew that if the Bullets kept playing this type of game, it would be a rocky road. In essence, the only thing that hurt

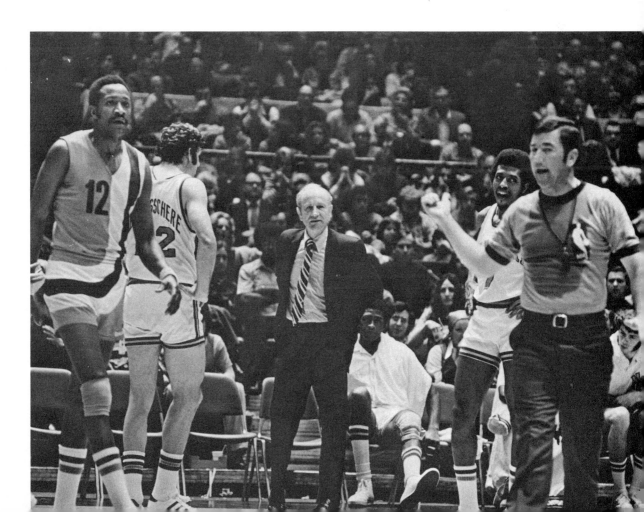

them was they didn't have that good a bench. Their first five men played a whale of a ball game.

I remember, after the game, Clyde saying to me he didn't think that either team in this series would break 100 points, not with the defense that was being played.

In the first game, it's like a boxing match where the fighters come out at the bell and try to lure each other into mistakes, while feeling out their opponent. There is usually a lot of give and take.

Earl told the reporters that he likes to think of the regular season as just the prelude to the playoffs. Maybe that was because he was hurt a lot that year, but I know you can't have that attitude and be the ballplayer that Monroe is, day-in, day-out.

In any case we needed a performance like that from Earl, and I believe he needed it also. During the season, more than once, I'm sure that Earl felt Clyde's shadow looming over him. It's tough for an All-Star, one of the most prolific scorers in pro ball, to be traded and have to take a back seat. In a way, that's just what happened to Monroe.

Aside from Earl's great game, the most heartening thing that happened was that our defense really came alive. We played as a team, dropping off, helping out, picking up the man coming down the middle.

It was truly a team effort . . . as was Baltimore's. I think we were fortunate to be at home for that first one. I still wasn't moving as well as I wanted, encumbered with that big leg brace, but I was happy because we won and I felt I had made a contribution.

While we got the big jump—winning that first game is so important in a best of seven series—the Celtics remained idle. They had a couple of extra days before they would meet the Hawks in the other Eastern Division clash.

Although we were up a game, I'm sure that everyone on the team would agree there was no reason for overconfidence. The Bullets were a most worthy foe.

The second game was also played at the Garden and, man, it was a shocker. We came out ready for a tough, defensive-minded Bullet team and what we saw was the old, wide-open express.

Dave hit a couple of long jumpers in the first quarter. I connected on three more, and pretty soon Unseld and Hayes were on us like wallpaper. We took them outside and left the middle open. Then it really happened . . . Earl and Clyde put on one of the greatest shows I've ever seen.

The Bullets are a tough team. We really had to work hard for our shots.

With nobody in there to block the lane, our backcourt men just kept driving. They'd go all the way, score, get fouled by a smaller man, or they'd pull up for that short jumper inside the foul line. It was fantastic.

Before the series started, Baltimore boasted that its backcourt of Archie Clark and Phil Chenier were the match of any pair in the league. But after two games, there was no comparison.

On defense, Frazier and Monroe stole everything in sight, and on offense it seemed that the only thing that would stop them would be to call the game because of rain. Certainly, the Bullets just weren't capable this night.

The biggest battle on the court was probably between Earl and Clyde for scoring honors. Monroe played thirty-six minutes and wound up with thirty-two points; Clyde added twenty-nine, and we never gave Baltimore a chance to catch up.

Hayes elected to go back again into the shooting role and wound up with only seven rebounds. Clark had an off-game, but Chenier surprisingly scored twenty-seven points. I say that because Chenier wasn't primarily a scorer then, although he is now.

We had beaten the Bullets by twenty points, 123–103, and the decision was never in doubt. I was satisfied with my game also, since I scored sixteen points and grabbed ten rebounds. I felt I helped in dragging Hayes and Unseld outside. I played thirty-six minutes and felt good.

The crowd was yelling for us to pour it on and Red used every player. The fans at the Garden were amazing. Every one of the starting team received a standing ovation. I can't tell you how much that means to a player. It's like someone patting you on the back and saying, "Job well done."

There's no other feeling like it in sports. After all those hours of hard work in the schoolyards and Boys Clubs, after hustling your way through college, and the learning stages of professional basketball, you get this recognition and sign of appreciation. It's unique and I don't think I'd trade it for anything.

Now, with two big wins, we should have had the momentum to knock the Bullets out but the series was going to move to the Civic Center in Baltimore. We knew that the Bullets were going to be tougher there.

We were getting steady performances from Dave and Bradley. Bradley was playing a good defense and his moves without the ball kept the team running, but in the matchups he was being beaten in the scoring column by Mike Riordan. There was some speculation that Lucas or Jackson might take over in Bill's spot.

But Red, as well as the rest of the team, had a lot of confidence in Bradley. We'd just have to work harder on Riordan, that's all.

The press corps continued to allude to the fact that we were perhaps a one, possibly two-man team, but nothing could have been further from the truth. Every man does his job on our squad. It's just that some are counted on for scoring more than others. Some are counted on for rebounding. Bradley, for instance, sets the pace of the game; Dave is tough rebounding and has a good basketball mind. Many of the plays we use on out-of-bounds originate with DeBusschere. Luke is primarily a shooter, who can hold his own rebounding; Jackson is a defensive artist. We all do our own thing and try to put it together. For the first two games of the series everything worked, but we still were not going to take Gene Shue's ball club lightly.

We had four days off before playing Baltimore again and we tried to keep track of the other playoff results. Boston had swept their first pair of games with the Hawks relatively easily; Los Angeles had dunked the Chicago Bulls twice and Golden State had split a pair with Milwaukee and Kareem Abdul-Jabbar.

We forced Baltimore to play our game in the third contest, and although it was close, 103–96, I venture to say that we were in control all the way.

If the Bullets hadn't gotten an exceptionally good performance from the Big E, thirty-six points, we would have run away with it. All of our starters finished in double figures, and we played a tough, never-let-up defense that shut off Baltimore every time it appeared to get close.

Finally, it looked like we were going to be able to sweep the series. That would certainly be a break if we could do it, because we'd need all our reserve strength against the Celtics-Hawks winner.

Everything was going right and we were riding the crest. A few of the guys on our team thought it would be a laugher in the fourth game, because the Bullets were demoralized. The only thing we really had to guard against was overconfidence.

We had played so well even Red couldn't scowl. Everyone was moving constantly at both ends of the floor. We hit the

Bill Bradley had a good series after starting slowly against Mike Riordan.

open man for a good many free shots and, very importantly, Bradley reestablished himself in the matchup with Riordan. He worked his way into the clear for that soft shot of his and wound up with twenty-three points and five assists. Mike had fourteen points. It was all a lot of fun.

It was truly a professional showing. We communicated with each other, picking up on defense, helping out all the time. The Bullets just didn't seem to do that. They didn't play poorly. We just had what I consider one of our most outstanding games.

Encouraging was the fact that we opened up in the third quarter. That was something we were unable to do most of the season. And we made it look easy.

Most of the experienced guys on the club hadn't even thought about a sweep. You just don't do such things against a tough club like Baltimore, but now Dave and I saw it as a distinct possibility. After all, we hadn't thought we'd be three games up so fast.

I remember Gene Shue saying he thought his team had played well enough to beat the Knicks on most nights. That might have been true, but we had it that night and there was no taking it away.

What's more it no longer was a Walt Frazier-Earl Monroe show. Bradley had twenty-three; Dave, nineteen; and I had sixteen.

I felt exceptionally well that night and I asserted myself in the last quarter, scoring eight points on a couple of dunks and a pair of jumpers. I was moving much better now, and, again, I played thirty-six minutes.

Aside from the offensive showing, I was able to switch off on defense and blocked a couple of shots, one a Wes Unseld jump shot, which brought a roar from the crowd. I was pleased with our showing. I think we all were. After all, there's only one way you can beat 3–0, and that's to end the series with a shutout.

That's what we tried to do a couple of nights later, but Baltimore just wouldn't go for it. They almost blew us off the court, 97–89.

Gene Shue had made a few adjustments in his lineup. He shifted Wes Unseld to play me head-on and moved Hayes onto DeBusschere. He also switched the backcourt match-ups, having Clark move onto Frazier with Chenier guarding the Earl.

I don't think it was the changes in the lineups, however. There's just too much pride on a team like the Bullets to

go down four straight. Maybe we were looking ahead a bit to the finals of the Eastern Division playoffs, I don't really know, but that time we looked ragged.

Clyde and Luke were the only ones who looked consistent with seventeen and fifteen points, respectively. Meanwhile Elvin poured through another thirty-four points; Clark had twenty-one and Chenier eighteen. But I think it was Unseld who was the key.

He kept coming at the boards, getting the outlet pass and Clark was maneuvering some kind of running game. They sunk us with accurate shooting from long and short range.

The Bullets worked around Wes on offense, too, using his muscle to their advantage. Hayes and Clark kept bombing while Chenier and Unseld pumped toward the basket.

Baltimore had an aggressive defense and caused an unusual amount of turnovers. Clyde and Earl were having difficulty getting the ball over the mid-court line, and, consequently, were forcing some poor shots. I guess it was only natural that we should have had a letdown.

Red only used me eighteen minutes, mostly spot play, and I only got five points. I also had a tough time trying to contain the storming Unseld. The Bullets thought we were having too easy a time on Wes for the first three games and began to look for him again on offense. He's a tough man, and although he had only nine points, he set up a lot of scores. The whole trouble was the Bullets had forced us to play their game—more of a one-on-one affair than a team effort.

Listening to the news, we heard that the Hawks were still battling the Celtics and the series was tied at two games apiece. That was a bit of relief in itself.

I was disappointed in my performance in the fourth game. I wasn't able to move the way I wanted, nor was I having a good time trying to keep Unseld blocked out. If my season was one of ups and downs I'd have to say this was one of the valleys. But now we could look towards going home to Madison Square Garden.

The word out West was that Golden State and the Bucks were tied at two games, and so were the Lakers and the Bulls.

We received a fine welcome from the New York fans when we stepped out on the Garden floor for the start of the fifth game. It wasn't as easy a game as the score might indicate. We won by ten, 109–99, but at the end of three

Earl the Pearl consistently got the clutch basket during our series with the Bullets. He also beat the rap that he doesn't play defense.

quarters we were up by only a field goal and the lead had changed hands almost more times than one could count.

This was the fourth time in the last five years that we had met the Bullets in the opening round of the playoffs, and we've been lucky enough to knock them out each time. To me, they remain a tough ball club. We've had better luck against Boston than Baltimore, and I never look forward to an easy night against the Bullets.

I think the major difference between the Bullets and our club is that we are much stronger on the bench and are able to wear them down somewhat. This was never more apparent than in the fifth game when Phil Jackson replaced Bradley and scored thirteen points while doing a whale of a job on the Big E defensively.

Throughout the series we had depended on a lot of different players and it paid off. In each game a different guy took the starring role. Clyde and Earl had a fantastic series. Dave was his usual dependable self; Bradley gave a steady performance, and I was pleased with my own contributions.

We were also lucky in that Atlanta was pushing the Celtics much harder than expected. They might be weary after a rough opening round.

All in all, I'd say our stingy defense and deep bench gave us the series against Baltimore. Our third and fourth quarter performances were encouraging, another sign of bench strength.

Earl again led the scorers. In the final contest, he had twenty-six points.

The Big E, who had had a great series in his own right, thought we'd have a tough time with Boston because the Bullets had kept the pressure on us in the opening round. I thought about that and kept telling myself we were ready to go . . . all the way.

I think Elvin was upset because Phil had all but cut him off from the offense, playing in front of him and not allowing the Bullets' guards to get the pass through. His point may have been valid, but we wrapped up our series in five games, while it took Boston six and Golden State six, and the L.A.-Chicago set went seven games.

I was concerned that we might get too much rest after finishing off Baltimore. We had to wait for the conclusion of the Celtics-Hawks round, which meant a week of rest before meeting the Celts. That's something you worry about when you're going good. There is always the possibility we would lose that fine edge. But hopefully, we'd hang in there.

We are good perimeter shooters, but once in a while, Clyde will penetrate that defense like it was butter. Baltimore found that out the hard way.

Archie Clark teamed with Wes Unseld and Elvin
Hayes to give Baltimore a tough fast break.

Up Against Boston's Celtics

With the best record in the league, Boston received the home court advantage for the first game. That also meant the seventh game would be at Boston Garden if one was needed. That's worth at least six to ten points, I'd say.

That was no excuse, however, for the way we were clobbered that first game. The Celts completely outplayed us and whomped us, 134—108.

Instead of coming on strong with the fast break, they used a more patterned offense, slowing the ball down and using picks and rolls. Our defense was cut to shreds as Jo Jo White penetrated, swerved and completely outmaneuvered Frazier and Monroe. Cowens had fifteen rebounds, many on the offensive board.

If you're going to get beaten, perhaps it's better to lose by a wide margin than by one or two points, especially when you start second-guessing yourself.

Although White seemed to be all over the court he had a lot of help. John Havlicek, the old pro and maybe the best clutch player in the game, registered twenty-six points and handed out eleven assists; Don Nelson played nineteen minutes and posted twenty-one points. He's another veteran who's always been tough on us. Cowens had eighteen, as did Don Chaney; and Paul Silas was real tough in rebounding.

The Celtics and Tom Heinsohn had a great day. And the Boston fans, some 16,000, were already beginning to compare this team with those of Red Auerbach's great teams of the past.

Havlicek had said before the game, "Every one is a struggle, and I always prepare myself for the worst." He didn't have to that day. We were down thirty-five points with three minutes to go. Just to show you how frustrating it can be, we shot seventy-four percent in the first quarter and were losing, 34—30.

I was going to have to react a lot quicker against Cowens, a big tough redhead, who has the moves and speed of a forward. He's got a good shot, can drive, and is a bull under the boards.

Between Luke and myself we had only fourteen points and eight rebounds. We were not going to win like that. Some of the Boston fans made that painfully clear; some were even abusive, throwing cigar and cigarette butts at our bench.

The Celtics' movement was excellent and we weren't stepping up to the screens they were setting. They beat us

In game number three with the Celtics, usually mild-mannered Bill Bradley tangled with Don Nelson. Both the referee and I restrained the contestants from any real disruption of the game.

every time. It certainly was a sobering experience. Now we'd get the chance to show what we could do at home.

A freakish thing happened—a complete about-face. We went out, took charge and rapped the Celtics, 129–96. It wasn't even close. It looked like a rerun of the first contest with the two teams switching uniforms.

From the moment we stepped on the floor, the whole place erupted in a frenzy of emotion. The intense rivalry between the two teams is incredible. The fans began their applause with the pre-game introductions and the pitch built so high that the crowd noise drowned out the National Anthem. It may have been unpatriotic, but it sure is loyalty to the team, and we really appreciated the backing after a twenty-six point loss two nights earlier.

Dave started the whole thing off with two steals and seven straight points. He was really charged up. All the guys on the club were psyched up. This was a big game. It was only one game, but it was important on which side of the ledger you would write it—in the winning or the loss column.

If we went down by two and gave Boston the momentum, it would really be tough coming back. But we won and again we were even with five games to go.

Our defense came through again. We applied a lot of pressure, especially in the backcourt, and I think we had them rattled for a while.

Cowens collected three quick personals by the middle of the second period, and we were just beginning to open up. When Heinsohn decided to give his center a rest, we poured it on and went eighteen points up, 46–28. Boston never did get back in the ball game.

Clyde with twenty-four points and Dave with nineteen stood out, but we had eight men in double figures and played the bench most of the last quarter. I had a relatively good game, scoring ten in just seventeen minutes. I also was able to contribute to the team by bottling up the middle. That way we held the high-scoring Cowens to eleven points. Havlicek had twenty-one tallies and White fifteen, but both had off-shooting nights.

They were forced to gun from the outside. Havlicek said afterwards, that our defense was what won our ball game. And he is right. That's basic. That's just what Red wants . . . and it works.

But you really couldn't get too high from the euphoria following the second game. We knew there was still a long way to go and it wasn't going to be that easy to cut off that

Boston fast break, that tough scoring machine which had run through the league.

Jackson's play again was a source of encouragement. He played well, defensively, and wound up with sixteen points. Bradley and Luke had ten each; Earl tallied twelve; Deano scored eleven. Man, that's a well-balanced attack.

But as Dave said, "These two teams are too good to be beaten by thirty points. I don't think you'll see another big spread in the series."

It was back to Beantown for the third game, and it appeared as if the fans had become basketball fanatics . . . either that or maybe we were getting the spillover of Bruins fans, since that National Hockey League team had been eliminated in its playoff bid.

The third contest, which was shown on national television, was a scramble right from the start. We won it, 98—91, thanks to an outstanding job from two guys who usually are on the bench, Jackson and Dean Meminger.

Both teams came out using the fast break and it seemed like we were going to run ourselves into a state of exhaustion. The pace was tremendous and the lights from the TV cameras didn't help.

Earl Monroe got a hip pointer in a collision with John Havlicek and Dave DeBusschere complained of leg cramps and dehydration. But Meminger did a fine job in place of Earl, getting the step on Chaney and moving the ball club with the expertise of a ten-year veteran. Unfortunately, his value doesn't show up in the box scores.

Jackson kept Havlicek under wraps, although John finished with a game-high twenty-nine points. Bradley was in early foul trouble and Luke played quite a bit at forward.

We were more aggressive on defense, more physical than we had been in the first contest at Boston. We were going for the ball and getting it. The decisive action came in the second period when we outscored the Celts, 29—17. We left the court at halftime breathing fairly easily with a 58—46 lead. Boston came back with Cowens and Havlicek spearheading the attack, but a pair of field goals by Bradley and another by Clyde and we pulled away.

I had a real good game, although Cowens managed twenty-seven points. He's a tough man to stop. But in thirty-four minutes, the most action I had seen in the Boston series, I scored eighteen points and pulled down eleven rebounds. I had more fluid movement than at any time since the start of the playoffs.

111

With the Celtics' running game in good shape, we needed the old pro, Dick Barnett, to help us a bit. Although he didn't see that much action in the series, he was a steadying influence. He's a real student of the game.

I'd say this one belonged to the bench, though—Jackson and Deano. They did some job. We all felt pretty good about going back to New York with a 2–1 advantage. That might neutralize any seventh game edge.

The Garden was rocking again. No organist ever had a tougher time playing The Star-Spangled Banner. And we responded with one of the most sluggish performances turned in all year. That we won was amazing in itself.

At first, we thought we'd have an easy time, since John Havlicek was going to sit this one out. He claimed he couldn't use his right arm, since he had been injured in Boston two nights before. But the absence of Hondo in the lineup just spurred Tom Heinsohn's team to put out that much more.

They quickly darted out to a 48–37 lead before the intermission. The game was marred by fouls, and what Heinsohn refused to call anything other than poor judgment on the part of the officials.

But the calls didn't all go one way, something Heinsohn failed to realize when he told reporters afterward that a visiting team has to be ahead by at least twenty points going into the final quarter in New York.

It took us a pair of overtimes and some great play by Clyde and Dave to pull it out, but we managed. Our defense took hold in the fourth quarter, limiting the Celts to seventeen points, while we scored thirty-three ourselves. And we needed all of them . . . just to tie.

White and Cowens came right out and started to do a job on us. JoJo was popping from the outside and hitting. Then he'd drive the baseline. He was all over the court, and they were getting the ball to him.

Cowens was coming out to the top of the key—shooting those line drive jump shots and then moving me back for the hook shot. I was forced to leave the lane open for other traffic.

While the Celts were cracking on all cylinders, we looked listless on offense. We just couldn't seem to mount an attack. After such a poor first half, we came back with the grand total of fourteen points in the third session. But when the curtain came down, it was still a victory. It certainly wasn't one of our better efforts, but we'd take it anyway.

Dean and I fouled out, and Red substituted the rookies, Bibby and Gianelli, and they really came through for us. Bibby opened up the offense with his driving ability and

There were only two seconds left in game number four and Jackson forced the game into overtime by harassing Don Nelson.

John just threw his weight around finally drawing the sixth foul on Cowens. When Cowens went out of the game in the second overtime, Boston's back was broken and Heinsohn became upset over the officiating.

With the score 89–87 in favor of Boston, Clyde tossed in the tying score. He wound up with thirty-seven for the night. Dave again had a good steady game contributing twenty-two points; Bradley had thirteen and I posted ten with nine rebounds. I found myself unable to move with the much smaller Cowens. I was getting boxed out and run around. I wouldn't say I played well, although I think I made some big plays.

One of the more important things was that I was able to pace myself through forty-two minutes of action. Luke was ineffective against the much stronger, more physical Cowens, and it had to be my job to shut off the big lefthander. I don't know if we were lucky that Hondo didn't play. Nelson turned in a very good game for them.

In any case, we had a two game lead after four confrontations, and we were relatively happy.

Sure we were ahead 3–1, but we knew it wasn't going to be a tea party trying to finish the series in Boston Garden. Personally, I had had enough of the fine New England food for the year, and was hoping we would either win the deciding game right then or, at the very least, in New York the next time the two squads would meet.

But neither was to be the case. We had to go the full seven against those stubborn Celts. This was turning out to be a tough playoff—from the very first game against Baltimore through the finale with Boston—there was no letup. I was hoping that the strain wouldn't overtake the Knicks.

The fifth game was really rough. The Boston fans watched a see-saw battle for four periods. The Celts emerged with a 98–97 victory. Dave sure seemed prophetic with his line about the margin of victory. It was narrowing with each game.

Havlicek, his shoulder still bothering him, was ready to go. He played with one arm, but hit the shots when needed. He was their inspiration. Although his time was curtailed to thirty minutes, he had eighteen points. Not too bad for a one-armed man from Ohio State.

Frazier is more than just a shooter. He gets the rebound, steals the ball and sets up the open man.

117

Tempers flared in the Boston series.

It was Cowens who *really* burned us. Boston led for three quarters by a hair-thin margin. Fights among the fans broke out all over the arena. I don't know whether it was the New Yorkers or Bostonians who were responsible for the melee, but eggs and soda pop bottles flew, and fists were popping up all over the place.

Boston played a good, strong defensive game, and forced us into making mistakes. We were unable to work a man free for the good percentage shot from fifteen feet in.

But we kept running with them, hustling, playing in spurts. Finally, we caught them for what looked like the deciding basket. Bradley hit it with sixteen seconds to go— a soft jumper that parted the nets.

Now all they would have time for would be an out-of-bounds play. They tried to get the ball to JoJo, although we figured the natural for the score would be Cowens, who already had thirty-two markers and was playing a fine all-around game.

JoJo rushed his jumper and it came up short, far short. We were all waiting around to grab the ball off the rim, but it never got there. Paul Silas grabbed the ball out of thin air, went up for the shot and was fouled. He's not that good a shooter, but he had three to make two, and he sank them without fanfare, a veteran doing his job.

Silas had been playing quite a game. He had twenty rebounds and was rough on defense. He also hit a couple of timely baskets for the Celts. He had proven that Boston was more than just White and Cowens and Havlicek. As a whole they were a tough team.

We set up the final shot for Frazier or Bradley with seven seconds on the clock. Boston was all over them and I found myself with no one to get the ball off to. I took the jumper, a forced shot over Cowens, who never let up, his arms moving like a windmill all the time. The shot fell short and that was the ball game. Now the pressure would be on again, but at least we were going home.

Everything was at fever pitch. The excitement in the Garden was like electricity. The fans were just waiting for us to put the bow around the Eastern Division championship as they sang "Good-Bye Boston, we hate to see you go." They were confident that this team from New York, the one that had kept battling all year despite some crippling injuries, would put the final mark on the Celtics this day and go on to face Los Angeles in the NBA championship finals.

120

The Celtics, Dave Cowens in particular, thought differently. Although Havlicek was dressed, he didn't play much. His shoulder was obviously hampering his scoring. However, every time you looked up it seemed as if Cowens was there, squirting through the defense, going over the outstretched arms, ducking under the guards, muscling on the boards, outrunning men he had no right to beat in a foot race.

In this game Dave Cowens came of age. He had always had all of the necessary equipment, but in the past he had shown signs of immaturity. He would blow sky high if he got a few early fouls called on him. He'd push back if he thought he was wronged on a call, picking up an added personal foul. But this night he was cool and graceful as a ballet dancer, and he turned in one of those performances that can't be captured on canvas.

Cowens has the competitive fire of a Havlicek with possibly more natural ability, by which I mean he can hurt you in more ways. Cowens could move out and be a top NBA forward if Heinsohn had anybody else who could play the pivot. He's strong and quick and smart. And he showed all of these things in the sixth game.

In football, I guess, it's called the animal instinct. That doesn't necessarily refer to hurting another man . . . just going all out.

Cowens wound up with twenty-six points as the Celts scored a 110–100 victory. He was unrelenting, as JoJo White, Paul Silas and Don Chaney worked the entire offense around their pivotman.

I had a bad game. I just did not have the speed to go with Cowens. I felt as if I was anchored to the floor and, for one of the few times in my career, I was booed in the Garden. But I don't think there's a center in the NBA that could have contained the Celtic lefty that day.

He and White went the full forty-eight minutes and combined for fifty-one points. Silas picked up a lot of dumpy shots and wound up with eighteen; Chaney had fourteen, and Nelson, twelve. It just wasn't our game.

The Celtics came out running, with White controlling the tempo of the game. White was bringing the ball down, pulling up and hitting the jumper from twenty-five feet out. If we moved up on him, he'd drive down the middle and either shoot or hand off to Chaney, trailing. It was a great bit of playing on JoJo's part.

While it seemed as if Boston was burning up the nets, we couldn't get our offense untracked. Frazier finished with twenty-nine and Monroe with twenty-two points, but I was only able to get four. We had no inside threat. Even Dave had only ten; while Bradley was four for twelve, far below the regular percentages.

We lost the game in the final quarter. That was something to think about, since we sometimes depend on our depth to pull us through in those last twelve minutes. But this time it did not work.

Now we were ready to take the game to Boston. We started the finale with DeBusschere playing Cowens, since he's quicker than either myself or Luke. But we kept switching it. I'd take him for a while and so would Lucas. The main thing was to keep the ball away from him.

Before the game everyone was calm. We knew what had to be done, and just how much time we had to turn the trick. We're a veteran team, and I think we kept our poise more than the Celts. The pressure was there, naturally, but most of us had been through it before.

The important lesson learned in the previous game was that Havlicek with his torn shoulder muscles was no longer much of a threat. We would have to concentrate on stopping Cowens and White.

So I sagged on the big center and kept Earl on top of JoJo throughout the opening quarter. We were still down, 22–19. Then Red brought in Deano to replace Monroe and it seemed to make us a different ball club. Earl had been having a great playoff, but what we needed at this point was primarily a defensive player. Deano has great speed and fast reactions, and my roommate is quite a student of the game. He knew JoJo's moves as well as White himself. He always seemed able to anticipate where White would be. He also gave us a faster movement up the court, allowing more time to set up the patterns.

From the time Dean came into the game, we took charge. Meminger kept talking, trying to catch White unaware. He moved the whole team, and once again, the bench had made a major contribution to our victory, 94–78.

Dave was taking the outside shot away from Cowens and I was blocking him inside. That way we also clogged the driving lanes while Deano was tormenting White in the backcourt.

The seventh game against the Celtics. We were confident we'd win even though we were playing on Boston's home court.

My roommate, "Dean the Dream," stood out defensively, holding JoJo White below his average in the final game of the Boston series.

We took our halftime lead of 45–40 to the dressing room, and by the end of the third quarter we had just about put the decision out of reach at 72–57. Actually, all we did was play our own game. We ran when we had the chance, got the good percentage shot and took advantage of the Boston turnovers. But I think it was Deano's day to howl.

On top of his great defensive play and generalship on the court, he managed to bag thirteen points. Clyde had twenty-five; Bradley and I registered fifteen each; Dave, thirteen, and Jackson chipped in nine.

Nobody can really say what would have been the result of the Boston series had Havlicek been able to go all out for seven games. I think our ball club would have won anyway.

In the final contest, it was our tough aggressive defense combined with good movement on offense which knocked the Celts out of the box. They are, however, a team truly worthy of respect.

With Bradley and Luke, in a happy moment.

128

The plane ride to L.A. was rather casual. We all knew what had to be done.

We Meet-and Beat The Lakers

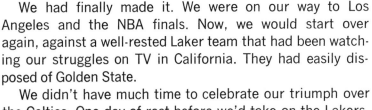

We had finally made it. We were on our way to Los Angeles and the NBA finals. Now, we would start over again, against a well-rested Laker team that had been watching our struggles on TV in California. They had easily disposed of Golden State.

We didn't have much time to celebrate our triumph over the Celtics. One day of rest before we'd take on the Lakers.

Los Angeles had to be one of the most devastating teams in the league, what with the likes of Wilt Chamberlain, Jerry West, Gail Goodrich, Bill Bridges and Jim McMillian. They had the strength and the savvy to make you play their game.

We had come a long way and with the time difference we didn't even have a chance to work out before taking on the Lakers. All we were able to do was watch some of their films. We knew there would be changes for our series, but we weren't able to set anything up. The Lakers took a 59–49 lead at halftime.

Naturally, we began to adjust and looked like a different unit in the second half. I've always seemed to have pretty good luck against Wilt. He has a certain style of play. Once you know it you can anticipate his moves. He'd been playing a bit rougher in recent games, but essentially he was used as the post man, feeding off to West, Goodrich and McMillian. He wasn't going to hurt you with his shot, unless he was alone, underneath.

With Wilt in the middle, the Lakers were playing a one-man zone with four men switching off on defense. We'd been playing a tough defense, blocking a lot of shots and closing off the lanes. And Wilt also has been amazing, rebounding for Bill Sharman's ball club.

To combat Wilt's presence in the zone, we, or I, tried to get up the court as soon as possible after a basket or play. We'd have to try and wear him down somewhat. With luck, they'd get the ball to me. If Wilt was there I'd give off to either Bradley or DeBusschere trailing and they would have the open shot. If Wilt wasn't on me I'd just go right in towards the hoop. The big thing was to create a situation where there was going to be a free shot.

If I had the ball and was stopped by Wilt, I was still able to set a pick for Clyde or Earl. Red wanted to play everything by the book and that's what we did. Each time we looked at the films we anticipated how they'd react under a similar situation and we went on from there.

Wilt dominated the first game of the finals as the Lakers triumphed.

But all of that didn't come together for us in the opening minutes of the first game, which is evident by our 115–112 loss. We gained ground in the second half and began learning what we would have to do to beat this club.

Wilt played a great opening game. He intimidated everyone who came near the basket, and although he wound up with only twelve points, he had one of his better nights, pulling down twenty rebounds and knocking away seven shots.

He forced our men to hurry their shots and go up off balance. He completely stopped our penetration. At the end of three quarters, we were losing 95–79. Luke was ineffective against the muscular Wilt who refused to come out after him. Although he managed sixteen points on seven for fifteen, the Lakers had jumped out to a big enough lead to allow Wilt to roam under the boards. He made his presence known.

Our offense wasn't really crisp, and I blame a good deal of that on our lack of practice. We would have to bounce back, that's all.

We had six guys in double figures in the first game, but actually only Bradley, Monroe and Dave shot well. Bradley wound up with twenty-four points, constantly challenging Wilt on the drive, and Dave had twenty-three.

But it was Gail Goodrich's thirty; Jerry West's twenty-seven, and McMillian's twenty-four counters which put us away early. I played twenty-five minutes, scoring ten and grabbing only four rebounds. It was not what you'd call one of my better nights.

The key to our success has always been Coach Red Holzman's emphasis on defense. On the afternoon prior to the second game against the Lakers, we studied moving pictures of various games in which we could observe how effective our defensive moves had been and how we could improve on them. Some of the scenes we viewed are shown in the next several pages.

As much as most fans idolize the guy who puts the ball in the basket, defense has been the key to our game. We think we can stop anyone with Red's team-style defense, dropping off and helping out all the time. It has resulted in quite a number of blocked shots.

After a day's rest, we came right back and evened the series in Los Angeles, scoring a 99–95 victory as Bradley continued to play inspired basketball.

Luke and I started running even more on Wilt who was coming back slower on defense. We were able to set up the picks and hit that open spot on the floor.

I wouldn't call a 24–23 first quarter lead commanding, nor was our halftime advantage of 50–46, but we were doing what we knew had to be done, and we overcame some great shooting by West and McMillian to stay on top.

Red used a bit of strategy which worked, also, when Bill Sharman sent in seven-foot tall Mel Counts to get even more of a height advantage over us. We moved Bradley to play defense against Chamberlain. Red figured Wilt wouldn't go to the hoop too much, and he was right. I played Counts and went outside with him; Bradley pestered Wilt; and DeBusschere was sneaking in for the rebounds, getting that great position.

Bradley said later, "I don't really try to play Wilt. If he decides to go to the basket he can carry me and another guy with him." But Bill made his presence felt, scoring twenty-six points to lead the team.

I had eleven points and nine rebounds, and I again felt like we were playing that good team defense, our trademark. Wilt picked off twenty rebounds, but took only four shots and wound up with five points. They put all their apples in one basket with McMillian and West. Goodrich had an off-game. West dunked in thirty-two and McMillian twenty-six, but the rest of the Lakers contributed little with the exception of Wilt.

Our bench was also a source of enthusiasm. Jackson and Meminger helped us pull the win out. Phil came in and scored eight straight points, as he also kept an eye on Counts, and Deano shut off Goodrich, not allowing him to get set for the shot.

If you play Gail to the left you pretty much have him stopped and that's just what Meminger was doing. He overplayed him. If Gail went the other way, I'd pick him up, but in this manner, we stopped the toughest weapon in his arsenal—the pull-up jump shot.

We were a little weary but were also happy to be going back to New York with the series even at 1–1.

Wilt had completed the evolution from the most prolific scorer in the league's history to defensive standout. His shot blocking in the final series was reminiscent of Bill Russell.

It was good to go home with a clean slate, and although it seemed endless, it was like a new season.

Now we were back home, and had the psychological edge. We won the battle of the defenses, 87–83. What a game it was. You earn your pay in that kind of game. You are working all the time and are called on for that extra effort.

It was a good win for us, although we got off to a bad start. Looking up from a 16–7 score, we fought back, played team ball and overcame any height disadvantage.

It was by far my best playoff game since we won the championship in 1969–70. It was also a game of intellects with both teams constantly maneuvering.

In a low-scoring situation, you have to work twice as hard on defense. That's why both Luke and I were ready to do battle with Wilt. Each time we'd switch, we'd have a fresh man against him.

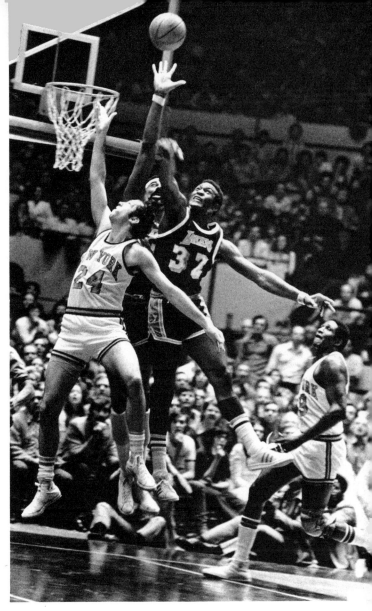

Bill Bridges lets fly against Bradley, while West manages to score 16 points in the second game despite his pulled hamstring.

147

The Lakers all played a tough defense, helping out underneath, switching off. They could afford to go for the ball, knowing Wilt was always there. This time West got called for the foul, however.

My shot was working and once again I felt like I was getting back into the rhythm of things. It had been a long time, and although I scored twenty-two points, I don't think that it was an individual show, by any stretch of the imagination.

Earl played an outstanding game, constantly swerving, turning, weaving, challenging Wilt with the short pop, and the double-action layups, and feedoffs. Earl's great ball handling was probably one of the major reasons I got so many open shots. I was really satisfied after this contest.

Our defense had looked great, and although Jerry West was hampered by pulled hamstring muscles in both legs, he did play and contributed sixteen points. The way we were going I don't think a healthy West would have made the difference in the outcome of the ball game.

In addition to my twenty-two points I had ten rebounds. Earl added twenty-one tallies, and Clyde, fourteen. McMillian was the Lakers' top scorer with twenty-two points. Everybody was looking for Wilt to go to the basket more, since Jerry wasn't able to go more than thirty-one minutes.

They had not gone to the big guy all year and he had his game set. They were unable to adjust to the situation, and didn't get the play from their bench that we got from ours. I think we just outplayed them. It was that simple. We were now leading the series 2–1, but that doesn't mean we thought we had it sewed up.

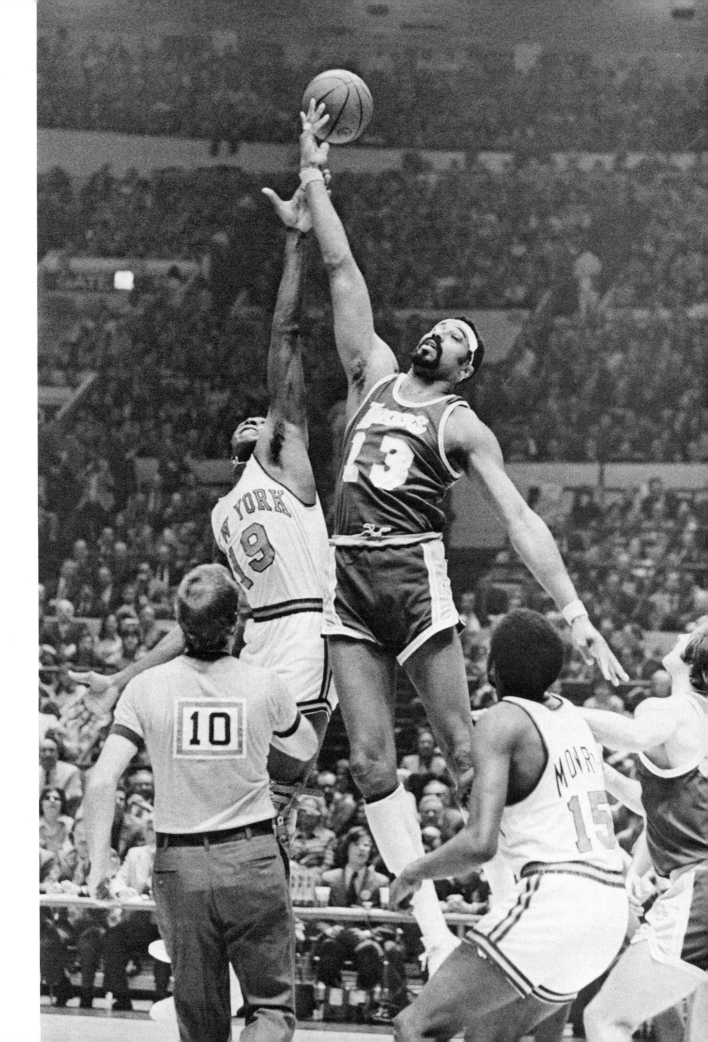

I think the fourth game of the series, played at the Garden, seemed like the longest one I was ever in. We just jumped out to a twenty-one point lead in the first half, and watched the Lakers shave and shave and dwindle that lead until we were pressing hard for the victory, which we finally achieved, 103—98.

We got the lead too early. Then we got cold and started playing too conservatively. That's not our style. They took advantage of it and suddenly their machine was running flawlessly.

As our lead kept disappearing, I asked myself over and over, "How much longer?" When I was getting a breather midway through the final quarter it looked like we were dying. I thought anything would be an improvement, but then I got lucky.

I replaced Luke and hit three straight jumpers off Wilt. I don't think he was expecting me to shoot so much, but I had regained a lot of confidence in my scoring power.

It was another good game for me. I felt I contributed on defense and I also scored twenty-one points on offense in thirty-two minutes of action. My movements were once again natural and fluid. I knew these last two games were a big plus for me.

A number of reporters asked me after the game if I was worried about Wilt going to the basket more often. If I had worried about him, I'd never have gotten any sleep. It's tough enough getting sleep as it is. The press kept throwing questions at me like what if Jerry's hamstring hadn't hampered him? All I can say is that West scored twenty-three points and that's not exactly the accomplishment of a cripple. We played our game and they played theirs.

Dave DeBusschere gave an outstanding performance, and it was the same story of a different man spearheading the team every night. Dave hadn't really had an outstanding game in the Laker series and he was certainly due. He's too great a player not to come up with one at clutch time.

Dave was hitting from the outside and playing a tough defense on McMillian, using the physical contact and brains that make him one of the premier forwards in the game. His shooting pushed us out to that early lead and he just kept popping, winding up with thirty-three points. Dave made the crucial play of the game late in the final stanza when Wilt and I went up for a rebound and couldn't get control. Dave grabbed the ball out of the air, drew the foul on Wilt and made the shot. The three-point play gave us a 97–92 lead with just a shade over two minutes remaining.

Clyde had fouled out and Earl was taking over as the ball control man. The Lakers wouldn't give up, however. They came back to 97–94, and West's shot made it 99–96 with thirty-one seconds left. At that point Wilt missed one of those rolling dunks and that was the game.

Dave collected four more foul shots for us. It certainly was an outstanding individual effort. To hold a team like the Lakers to ninety-eight points, the entire team must be tough on defense, strongly aggressive and also get some good breaks. It was a great feeling to come out of that game with a 3–1 advantage. We knew we would be going back to the West Coast, but we continued to believe in ourselves. We *could* beat the Lakers.

Dave grabbed a crucial offensive rebound in the waning moments of the fourth game, potted the foul shot and it was all over.

The Madison Square Garden crowds thrilled to the antics of Dancing Harry and his hexes. The fans are a great part of our "team game."

After the fourth game we took the plane to L.A. arriving at 6:25 A.M. New York time. At that hour (3:25 A.M. L.A. time) the Knicks were the only visible occupants of the airport terminal. That afternoon Dave said, "Let's win it in L.A. now." I was interviewed by Joe O'Day of The New York Daily News and Leonard Lewin of The New York Post.

The Final Test

The Knicks now had momentum, and we realized that we couldn't let ourselves be cradled into a false sense of security as in the series with the Celtics. We knew L.A. wasn't going to give an inch and we'd have to fight for everything we got.

It was not a must game, and it certainly wasn't as emotional as the 1970 encounter, but we knew it meant the whole season condensed into forty-eight minutes of play. If we lost, we'd have another chance, but if we could manage to put it in the win column I could go home and go fishing. I wanted it right then.

After we beat Boston, Red had said, "I know we're going to take it all." He really was confident. As a matter of fact, that's the cockiest Red has ever been.

He had his mind made up that we were going to come home with the championship banner and that was all there was to it. He had molded this team of superstars into a selfless, all-giving outfit. He had convinced us that the only way to win this game was for everybody to give their all 100 percent of the time. All of these thoughts went through my mind before the fifth game with the Lakers. I knew Red was right.

It had taken me quite a while to get flowing, and I might never play the way I did in 1969–1970, but I was finally moving towards the goals I had set for myself.

We took the court in Los Angeles, twelve guys determined to go into the record books. And we did, as the NBA champions, with a 102–93 verdict over a stubborn, never-say-die Los Angeles squad. It was not an easy game, but it was satisfying.

We were able to run more on the Lakers than we had on the Celts. With big Mel Counts, Wilt and Bridges in the lineup at the same time, the Lakers were saddled with three slow men . . . and we knew it.

163

That night we broke out to a 23–16 first quarter lead, but the Lakers kept pressing us and at halftime they had gained the advantage, 41–39. We played them tight all the way, giving them very little room to score, and our defense was outstanding.

Although the Lakers kept battling back, I think the only time we were really concerned was when Dave sprained his ankle with seven minutes to go. If we had lost that game and didn't have Dave for the remainder of the set, it would have been quite a blow.

We were in front 79–65 when Dave went out, and Phil Jackson took over. Jax did a fine job. I only regret that Dave wasn't on the floor when all the hoopla was coming our way.

Earl had twenty-three points, Bradley, twenty, and Clyde and I, eighteen each. I also nabbed twelve rebounds and thought my quickness was much improved.

Goodrich came on strong for the Lakers in the finale, with twenty-eight points, and Wilt began going to the basket with authority. He managed twenty-three points, but we had won the game and were the champions. And man, that's one of the most gratifying feelings in the world— to know you made your contribution to the winner.

With about seven minutes to go in the fifth and final game, Dave DeBusschere severely sprained his right ankle and was lost for the rest of the game.

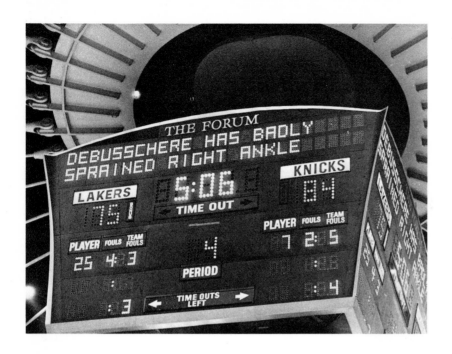

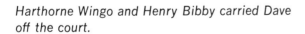

Harthorne Wingo and Henry Bibby carried Dave off the court.

We're the Champs

I was able to put it all together. I was satisfied with my defense, happy with my increased mobility and more consistent scoring. We wanted to take it in L.A. and we did. I also put Bradley on the rafters after the final buzzer—I felt that good.

After the Game

In the previous year, I hadn't known if I'd play again. After we disposed of the Lakers and I was voted the Most Valuable Player, I was astounded. We had so many good performances from so many good ballplayers that maybe there should have been twelve sets of keys for the car I was given. It was truly a team effort. I realize I've repeated that often but there is no way that I can overestimate the value of playing as a team.

It was in the fourth game in the five-game series that we had held the Lakers, who had averaged 110 points a game over the regular season, to less than 100 points. Five men on the court at once—five men hounding the player with the ball—five men switching—going to the backboards. It's the story of a great basketball team. I think we were a better club than the one which annexed the title in 1970.

We don't have to answer the questions of what if Havlicek wasn't hurt, what if West wasn't hampered. Just remember one thing, there's no asterisk next to the name of the champions of the NBA in 1973.

Red always told us, "Shooting is enjoyable; defense is hard work." It's characteristic of our coach. A basic philosophy, but so true. I maintain it was our defense that won the title for us.

There were a good many times during the season when I realized I wasn't helping the team. Red would move me into the role of a spot player, or try to get me more work. I never questioned his judgement.

Although I never really had any serious doubts about my knee, and I was interchanging four braces until the last month of the season, I never knew when I would be 100 percent. There was no way to tell.

I think if the MVP award had been for the entire playoff series, Clyde should have received it, but it was just for the finals, so I do accept it. I hope I did so with due modesty.

The strength of the Knicks is that when one guy is down, there's another player who pops up with a great game. I think we can adjust to any situation and do things other teams don't even try.

I'm certain this is the greatest team I have ever played for, and I'm equally sure it won't be the last championship team in New York that I'll have the honor of playing on.

I am going to try to forget all the ups and downs, the inconsistencies, I had during the course of the season.

After all, we won. . . . . .it was a great year.

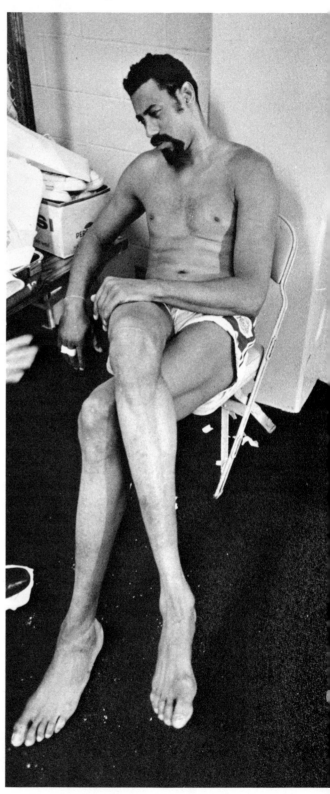

After the game—a bit of tonsorial touchup and an autograph for a young fan.

Dave's ankle kept him in the chair, but I didn't mind wheeling him. He'd been helping carry the team all year. He's a great competitor.

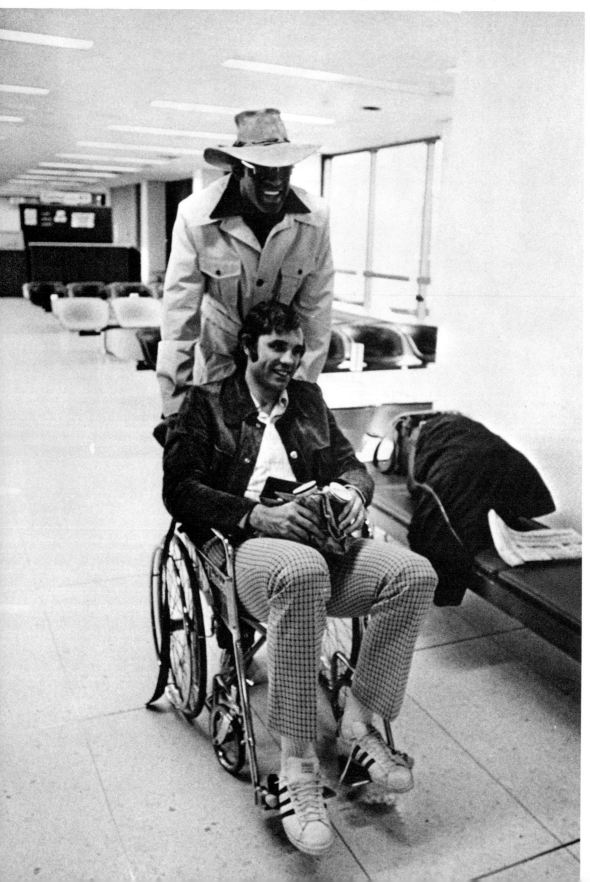

On the return air trip from Los Angeles, some of
us read, others played cards, while a member
of the press continued with an interview.

At a party for the team celebrating our victory we were able to unwind. Here (left) I am dancing with Gerri DeBusschere, Dave's wife.

The secretaries from the Knicks office (left to right Joanne Dinoia, Gwynne Bloomfield, Claudia Grandinetti) posed for a picture with me.

Bill Bradley shows his dancing technique.

New York's mayor, John V. Lindsay was on the scene after he declared New York Knickerbocker Day and held a reception for the team at City Hall. I was truly honored to be selected the Most Valuable Player by Sport. The crowds were wild with enthusiasm and finally broke through the police lines.

Another gratifying award I received in 1973 was the Maurice Stokes Memorial Trophy for the comeback of the year. Here Red Auerbach, renowned coach of the Boston Celtics, and now general manager, presents the trophy at Kutshers Country Club. My son Karl seems to be impressed with the ceremony.

While I was happy to accept the award of the automobile (which I, in turn, awarded to my mother), I think my words at the time expressed my true feelings: "It's been a gratifying year for all of us. Anyone of four or five players deserved the award and I personally would have voted for Walt Frazier. I'm a great fan of his . . . he's one great ballplayer.

"Also, I want to thank Mr. Irving Mitchell Felt, Mr. Ned Irish and Coach Red Holzman . . . they're the people that put the team together.

"I'm very happy for Jerry Lucas and Earl Monroe, both of whom are with a champion for the first time. I'm happy for my mother; it was she who said I could do it. Whatever mother says is usually right.

"Everybody thought the Celtics would run us off the court and Los Angeles was too strong for us. Well, L.A. wanted us and they got us. We're champions because we played well under pressure and it's the contributions made by the other players that brings you the award."

Man, life is just beautiful . . . again.

After the festivities were over I was able to return home to visit my parents in Bernice, Louisiana and do a little fishing. These are some snapshots I took of my mother and father and some other photos of the results of a relaxed morning of fishing.